It's A Mighty Thin Pancake

(that don't have two sides)

Andre:
I hope you enjoy
this (in spite of my tittle
ding towards the State (Chaules)
Ref

Rexford C. Early

Library of Congress Cataloging-in-Publication Data
Early, Rexford C.
It's a Mighty Thin Pancake (that don't have two sides)
by Rexford C. Early

ISBN: 0-9768052-7-8
13 # 978-0-9768052-7-4

new century
PUBLISHING

New Century Publishing, LLC,
36 E. Maryland Street,
Indianapolis, Indiana 46204

Cover photograph on the left, features the author
with John R. Gregg, Former Democrat Speaker
IN House of Representatives
and Former Interim President of Vincennes University

Quotes

Rex has always known how to take a good story and make it better. To paraphrase Samuel Johnson: "Truth is a cow which will yield people like Rex no more milk, so he has resorted to milking the bull." There is a fair amount of bull milking in Rex's life and in his book.

— Ann DeLaney, Former Democratic State Chairman and
Executive Director of the Julian Center

"I've met and heard about many Indiana Legends, Tony Kiritsis, Clarence Roberts, and countless others, but there's only one Rexford C. Early."

— John R. Gregg, Former Democrat Speaker
IN House of Representatives and
Former Interim President of Vincennes University

"Rex Early never bought a pencil from me, so I'm not gonna buy his book..."

— Ed Sagamore, Homeless pencil salesman
in downtown Princeton

"I've spent time w/ Seth Denbo, Ed Lewis, Orvas Beers, but none of them could swear like Rex"

— Billy Joe Whitesell,
Lawrence County Republican Activist

19 Rules of Politics

1. Don't get confused or let others get confused about which is the monkey and which is the organ grinder. Just because some dude has a mustache, that don't make him the organ grinder.

2. Don't ever vote for a man who has never peed in the backyard.

3. Don't ever monkey with another monkey's monkey.

4. Do not fish from the company pier.

5. Make sure that people know that this ain't your first rodeo.

6. Never grease the skillet until the bass is in the boat.

7. Don't try to be real humble. You probably ain't that great.

8. Always remember that fat people have feelings, too.

9. Remember that you might have been born at night, but not last night.

10. Don't trade old friends for new ones.

11. You must let people know that you didn't just get off the noon balloon from Rangoon.

12. Make sure you always dance with the one who brung you.

13. Never take a bone away from a skinny dog.

14. Read the book, *Plunkitt of Tammany Hall.*

15. Always remember: You might be important, but the number of people who will attend your funeral will be dictated by the weather.

16. There is just plain pocracy, and then there is *hypocracy: Hypocracy is bad.*

17. There's never a horse that couldn't be rode, and there's never a cowboy who couldn't be throwed. (Nothing is impossible.)

18. The cemeteries are full of "indispensible" men.

19. It's a mighty thin pancake that don't have two sides.

Table of Contents

Acknowledgements

Without the tireless efforts of the team of New Century Publishing in Indianapolis, this book would not exist. Constance Carlisle, the Project Manager, worked countless hours around the clock because of her love of books and the pride she takes in a job well done.

Betty Burgess helped the birthing of the book by taking handwritten pages from a legal pad and transforming them into the infant form of the manuscript.

Dan Fischer attended meetings, offered advice and suggestions, and will soon be moving copies and cases of the books around the state.

Teresa Artman had the challenge of keeping the voice of a hully-gully while constructing acceptable sentences and paragraphs and building them into the book you now hold.

Susan Harring did a wonderful job carefully crafting the look and feel of every page, cover to cover.

My friend, Dave Caswell, provided encouragement and optimism from our early conversations about the book until its release.

Introduction

Everyone wants to write a book—even goofs. I wanted my children and grandchildren to hear about some of the happenings that I thought were humorous and also hear about some (not all of them—just some) of my experiences.

I thought it was time to put some of them down on paper. I'm getting old. My good hip hurts. I can't hit a golf ball out of my shadow, and one of the members of my campaign for governor staff wrote a song entitled "He Thinks He Still Hears" (a takeoff on the country song "She Thinks I Still Care").

In fact, even though my hearing is perfect, I humored people and got some hearing aids, which reminds me. My wife came home from Sam's Club with a large jar of mixed nuts. I picked out a bunch of the cashews (my favorite), and the phone rang. I laid the cashews on the kitchen counter.

Later, I took a big handful of the cashews and was eating them when I bit down hard on what was a bad cashew. I liked to broke my tooth. I opened the back door and spit it out in the grass. Then I bit down on another "bad" cashew. It was hard as a brick. I spit it out and examined it. IT WAS ONE OF MY BRAND-NEW HEARING AIDS.

I had laid them on the kitchen counter, and they looked like cashews. After crawling around in the grass for 30 minutes, I found the other hearing aid.

Both hearing aids were heavily damaged and had to be sent back to the manufacturer. I told my audiologist the teeth marks were from my dog.

Back to the book—I could have spent the rest of my

life correcting my spelling and getting the exact dates that certain things happened. I did not do that (it really don't make a lot of difference if something happened in 1960 or 1961).

I have tried to relate the things in my life I thought were funny, especially in the political arena. Some of the things I wrote about like the American Battle Monuments Commission, I was serious as a heart attack. If anyone buys this book, the profits will go to the Seeds of Hope (a residential home for chemically dependent women) run by Father Glen O'Conner and Providence Cristo-Ray—a great charter school, run by Sister Jean, both are located on the west side of Indianapolis.

Chapter 1
The Early Years

Dad's Side: The Earlys and the Morans

The Early family came from Kentucky shortly after the Civil War. My grandfather, John Early, was in the Union Army. He joined the Army in Hawesville, Kentucky and was mustered out after the war ended in August of 1865, at the age of 18, at Cloverpoint, Kentucky. He moved to Indiana after the war and bought a small farm in Knox County, Indiana. The main crops were watermelons and cantaloupes. He married Sarah Moran, my grandmother, who was a red-headed Irishwoman from Knox County with a bad temper.

The Moran family was a large family. My dad told me that his Uncle Jim was referred to as "Uncle Jim Boar Nuts." He fathered nine children, and according to my father, would have fathered more if he hadn't read that every tenth baby born was Chinese.

Squirrely Early

My grandfather John was known to take a drink every now and then. He came home one day after a few drinks, and during the daily "cuss fight" with my grandmother, she read him the Riot Act about him not doing anything to eliminate the lice in the chicken house. John came up with the solution. According to my father, he soaked the chicken house with kerosene and burned it down to the ground: chickens, lice, and all. My father said that Grandpa John was prone to do things like that and was referred to in some circles back then as Squirrely Early.

Grandpa John had a bullet in his leg but he never told the family how he got it. My grandfather John died in 1920, 14 years before I was born.

Mom's Side: the Galloways

My mother's grandfather, Robert Fagg, was a colonel in the Civil War. He fought on the Confederate side, and I read an article in the Tazewell County History that he had a very distinguished military career. He was credited with capturing several Yankees in one battle. My grandfather, Jim Galloway (on my mother's side), was a native of Bluefield, Virginia. He was a deeply religious man and earned his living as the streetcar conductor in Bluefield.

When I was in the seventh grade, we lived in Bluefield. When the Ku Klux Klan had a march down the main street of Bluefield, my cousin (Jimmy) and I were spectators. Jimmy pointed out that one of the marchers all in their white sheets, was wearing a pair of shoes just like the ones that Grandpa had. What a coincidence!

Mom and Dad

My father, Henry Early, was born on his father's melon farm in Decker, a town just outside of Vincennes, Indiana.

He married my mother in Bluefield, Virginia when he was working over there as a salesman. Dad firmly believed that the collapse of civilization will be brought about by your liberal Democrats and socialist college professors. (He loved both Senator Joe McCarthy and Senator Bill Jenner.) Both were conservatives who were avid enemies of Communism.

He was 18 years old when World War I ended, and he was 41 years old when World War II started, so he missed being in the Army or in the service. After the Japanese bombed Pearl Harbor on December 7, 1941, I remember hearing Mom and Dad discussing the fact that he was going down to try to join the Navy. He went down, and they looked at his age—and they weren't taking 41-year-olds, even at that time.

I'm sure at one time my father was a proponent of Franklin Delano Roosevelt. Dad was a farmer during the Great Depression, and he felt Roosevelt was going to be the one who led them to prosperity. Roosevelt's theme was "helping the forgotten man." In fact, my dad named me after Roosevelt's domestic advisor, Rexford Tugwell. Later, it was whispered that Rexford Tugwell was a "little light in the loafers" and a Communist sympathizer. <u>I was named after a gay Communist</u>?

Two Republicans Are Born

Mom was pregnant with me when the bank foreclosed on their small melon farm that they owned in Knox County. An attorney named Floyd Young represented the bank and personally made the eviction. As it turned out after several years, when I was eight or nine years old, we were going to the same church as Floyd Young. Every Sunday, Dad would tell Mom, "There's that son of a bitch, Floyd Young!" I grew up thinking that "son of a bitch" was part of his name.

It was after they lost the farm that my dad became a very conservative Republican.

All Roads Lead to Indiana

After my folks lost the farm, Dad found a job in Missouri. Mom moved there to be with him, and when I was born, they were living in a small town called Albany, Missouri. My mother had some health problems when I was born and was unable to have anymore children, so I was an only child. After the Missouri gig, Mom and Dad moved frequently, always returning to Vincennes when things went really bad. Besides Albany, Missouri, I lived in Corbin, Kentucky; Jellico, Tennessee; Bluefield, Virginia; Wheatland, Indiana; and Oakland City, Indiana as well as Vincennes. When I was growing up, we seemed to always come back to Vincennes. Mom and Dad owned the house in Vincennes. It didn't have a furnace (just two coal stoves) or air conditioning, but it was always home.

Wheatland, Indiana:
The Foxhole and a Rat called Fred

When I was in sixth grade, Mom and Dad ran a restaurant in Wheatland, Indiana. It was during World War II, and the name of the restaurant was The Foxhole. During the war, meat was rationed, so we had to have another plan. The Foxhole's main course during the season included wild rabbit and squirrel. We served a lot of fish in the summertime. (What State Board of Health?) When I was 10 years old, Dad bought me a second-hand, single-shot .410 Winchester shotgun. There was an abundance of rabbits and squirrels in those days, and I got to be a good shot. (You better be, with a single-shot .410!) Dad was paying 50 cents for a cleaned rabbit, and I helped keep the inventory up. (I still have my .410.)

The Wheatland house did not have indoor plumbing. In fact, back then, very few houses had indoor plumbing in Wheatland. Not to be uppity, I would point out that we had a "double holer." I can remember thinking of the audio possibilities when both people had diarrhea. That never happened, but it was just a thought.

Like a lot homes with outhouses, we had what was known as a "shithouse rat." We named our rat, Fred. Fred was smart. All shithouse rats were smart. If I took my .410 out to the outhouse, you would never, ever see him. If I went to the outhouse without my shotgun, Fred would practically sit on my shoes! One day, I got Fred when I fooled him by taking my dad's .22 pistol instead of the .410 shotgun.

Fred and a Compliment for Senator Lugar

I remember back at the 1992 Republican convention in Dallas, Texas, we had a break period. I was sitting there, and a reporter who I didn't know, came up and wanted to talk to me. I was obviously from Indiana, as I was sitting in the Indiana section, and he wanted to know about Senator Dick Lugar. During the interview, I opined that Dick Lugar was smarter than a shithouse rat. Much to my chagrin, he printed that, and Marty Morris, Senator Lugar's Chief of Staff said that the senator actually read it in the Washington newspapers. He asked Marty what that phrase really meant.

I think that Marty succeeded in convincing him that was one of the highest compliments that Rex could give someone.

The Depot Café and Its Flying Spoon

After two years, we moved back to Vincennes, Indiana where Mom and Dad had a restaurant called The Depot Café. It was located 11 miles closer to the horse bookie establishment that my father visited every day. Our restaurant was also next door to the train station and was part of a building with a rundown hotel. The Depot Café was not what you would call a gourmet restaurant. The catch of the day was usually meatloaf. I was in junior high school, and I would come to the restaurant after school. I had certain chores that I was expected to do; and then, after doing them, I would go sit in a booth and do my homework.

Well, one day when the place was empty and Dad was behind the counter, a customer came in and asked for a cup of coffee. I heard him in a loud voice beckoning Dad. He was holding up his spoon and pointed out to Dad that the spoon was a little dirty. The spoon had some egg on it. Dad took the spoon, looked it over very closely, and then threw it clear across the room. Dad was yelling that, "Every son of a bitch that comes in here any more wants a clean spoon!", and he was tired of it. I think we lost a customer for good.

A Pitcher Is Born: The Depot Café Basement

My dad's sister, Aunt Lois, lived in Miami Beach, Florida. She worked for the city government. The city owned the baseball field where the Pittsburgh Pirates had spring training. Aunt Lois knew the city employees who maintained the field, and for several years, she would send me a big box of baseballs that the maintenance people found on the roof or out in the bushes. They would give them to Aunt Lois. I was the King of Baseballs in Vincennes, with a whole box of almost new baseballs every year. The building that housed the restaurant—I'm talking now about The Depot Café—also housed a hot-sheet hotel, and there was a joint basement under the restaurant and the hotel. It was a dingy place, and you guessed it: There were big rats in that basement. I would go to the basement and sit very still on a stool with my box of baseballs. When rats came out, I would try to hit them with a baseball. I hit several, and I think I even killed one. I credited this experience for me becoming a real-good high school and semi-pro pitcher when I got older. I think that basement is where I really learned to throw a slider, and it paid off certainly on being able to have good control.

After The Depot Café, we moved to Bluefield, Virginia, where my dad sold cars. In 1949, there was a coal miner union strike. When the miners stopped buying cars, we moved back to Vincennes.

Dad couldn't find work in Vincennes. A few months later, we moved to Oakland City. Nine months after that, it was back to Vincennes.

The Man in the White Stetson

If you liked to gamble, Vincennes, Indiana was a good place to live. We had three wide-open gambling joints, one complete with a ticker tape.

The Vincennes Ministerial Association decided that there was too much gambling in Vincennes. They sent a new, young minister into one of the joints who took notes.

My father was a gambler. He loved the horses, poker, gin rummy, or shooting craps. The preacher approached my father, who was playing gin, and asked whether there was a poker game around. My dad said, "No," but he could sure arrange one this evening if the new guy wanted to play. He probably thought the guy was a goof. (The guy probably was a goof.)

A couple days later, there was a full-page ad in the Vincennes Sun-Commercial, paid for by the ministers, in which they quoted my dad and described him to a tee, including his white Stetson hat. My mother was embarrassed to death. She was sure that everybody in Vincennes knew that the gambler with the hat was my father. Dad laid low for a little while.

My mother was a saint. Being born and raised in Virginia, she was the epitome of a southern lady. She never lost her southern drawl. I never heard my mother use any bad language. (However, her husband and son made up for that.)

My mother loved everyone. She worked almost her whole life. Her last job was at the Good Samaritan Hospital in Vincennes. She worked in the office there for 35 years. While she was there, the hospital put in a retirement plan except for two people they left out: the head nurse (Mrs. Cross) and my mother. Because of their age, it would have cost too much to include them. (So much for age discrimination.)

A few years later, I was downtown with my mother when the former chairman of the board of the hospital passed us. He was the culprit who excluded my mom. She spoke to him and told me what a wonderful man he was. I wanted to slap him upside the head and expressed that. Mother was a good Christian and forgave people. Not me.

Aunt Lois and the Candidate for Governor

Aunt Lois, who supplied me with baseballs, came back to Vincennes when her husband died. She had no children. In her later years, I took care of her. I moved her to Indianapolis for her last 10 years.

When I was running for governor in 1995–1996, I would stop in to see her at the Forum, where she lived. She was in her 90s and was getting a little confused. She would always say the same thing: "Where have you been?" Even if I had seen her that morning! One evening, I explained to her that I hadn't been there for a couple of days because I was running for governor.

She said, "My nephew, Rex, is also running for governor." When I told her I was Rex, she said, "You are not Rex! He's not fat!" I asked her who she was going to vote for, me or Rex, and she said, "I haven't made up my mind."

And They Passed the Torch

When Aunt Lois passed, at the age of 97, I had her buried in Vincennes. At her age, all her acquaintances and friends had gone. I bought the entire funeral home package, including the rent-a-preacher.

Just before the service, the preacher suggested I tell him a little bit about Aunt Lois, as he "liked to make his message somewhat personal."

He asked me whether her passing was unexpected. The lady was 97 years old! I told him, "Oh, yes. As a matter of fact, she had just played on the nursing home flag football team the day before she passed. Her passing was totally un-expected and a great shock."

My father was very sick in 1962, but he lived to see me sworn into the Legislature in January of 1963. The way he loved politics and the Republican party, my serving in the Indiana House made him very happy. He passed in March,1963, during that legislative session.

Chapter 2
Movin' On

Because my father was on the move (I think he wrote the song "Movin' On"), I went to three different high schools. In my sophomore year, I went to all three of them: Graham High School in Bluefield, Virginia; Lincoln High School in Vincennes, Indiana; Wood Memorial in Oakland City, Indiana; and then back to Lincoln High School in Vincennes.

One of the shining moments happened when I was a junior in high school. It was a down time at the Earlys, and our only mode of transportation was a hand-painted 1937 Ford. One evening, while Mom and Dad and I were in downtown Vincennes on Main Street, our car caught on fire. The flames were clear up to the light wires. Finally, the fire department came. It was really hard to be cool when your family's car was burning on Main Street. I think I told some of my friends, who gathered at the fire, that my Dad was tired of the car, and we just decided to burn it up.

With all the moving, I did not letter in algebra. After joining the class about half-way through the semester at Oakland City, I figured out that I was not going to be an algebra major. The algebra teacher might as well have been talking in Chinese.

Despite never understanding algebra and never taking any more math classes, I graduated from Lincoln High School as a member of the National Honor Society. Later, our newly elected Congressman Bill Bray gave me an appointment as his first alternate appointment to West Point. As it turned out, the principal got the appointment. I don't know whether I would have taken it or not. I probably wouldn't. Number one, I liked the Marine Corps. Number two, I liked girls. And number three, I didn't understand higher math and would have never passed the test.

I played football and baseball in high school and got athletic letters from all three schools. After high school, the St. Louis Cardinals scout, Runt Myer, invited me and about 20 other players from the midwest to Sportsman Park at St. Louis.

Early Retirement from Baseball

Mom and Dad went with me, and we even got our hotel room paid for by the Cardinals. It was a two-day tryout, and I heard there were two or three signed by the Cardinals. I wasn't one of them. I had good control, I had a good slider, and I could throw junk, but some of the other pitchers' change-ups were faster than my "blazing fast ball." They did hook me up with a team in Texas that might be interested, the Harlingen Caps in the Gulf Coast League.

I grabbed the Greyhound bus and joined them for three weeks. As it turned out, they were in a pennant race, and I just threw a lot of batting practice for them. Earl Caldwell, who pitched in the big leagues, was one of their pitchers. He had to be over 40 years old; his son was the catcher. We had a Fourth of July double-header in Brownsville,

Texas. We won both games, and their fans threw beer bottles at our team bus. Harlingen imported a couple of new pitchers and sent me packing. They did hook me up with a team in north Texas: the Sherman-Dennison Twins, in a D league. They were paying $85 per month. The next day after arriving in Sherman-Dennison, I got on the Greyhound bus and returned to my home and my girlfriend in Vincennes. That summer, I played baseball for various semi-pro teams around southern Indiana.

Goodbye, Vincennes

That fall, I was a student at Vincennes University, and I was tired of school. I had a falling out with my girl-friend (now my wife); I had several friends in the Marine Corps; and I had lost two of my friends, both of whom were Marines (Bob Fitch, an outfielder on my Oakland City High School baseball team; and Ace Edwards, a great, three-sport athlete from Vincennes). Their names are inscribed on the Korean War Memorial on Pennsylvania Street in Indian-apolis.

Semper Fi

Even though I had another month of school left, I en-listed in the Marine Corps. A week later, I was in Parris Island, South Carolina. Now Marine Corps Boot Camp ain't no picnic, especially in June and July at Parris Island. You throw in two mean-spirited, screaming drill instruc-tors (D.I.s Sgt. Pagerly and Corporal Veon—how could I forget them?), no sleep, 100-degree heat, and millions of sand fleas. It ain't a place you want to vacation.

After a week or two, I did have the satisfaction of

knowing I had taught my girlfriend a lesson she wouldn't soon forget. She just sent me pictures of her at the Vincennes swimming pool. I always wondered, "Who took the pictures?"

Marine Corps Boot Camp was structured so the faint of heart ain't going to make it. About half of those who started in our platoon graduated with our platoon. Some had been hurt or sick (two had heat stroke) and were dropped back to other platoons. Some went to a "slow learners" platoon; others were dropped. In those days, the Marine Corps wasn't so concerned about the DIs having a little physical contact with recruits.

Back then, we didn't have the "blue cards" that they have today, which read, "Sir, I want out." If you were in, you were in.

Two Very-Expensive Steam Irons

The pressure in Boot Camp was intense 24 hours per day. You had to be on your toes (like a midget at the urinal) all the time, and you had to <u>want</u> to be a Marine. One good thing happened at Boot Camp. On our first payday, our D.I. asked each of us for $5 to buy two steam irons so we could keep our dress uniforms somewhat pressed. With 50 or 60 people in our platoon, that was $250 or $300. The D.I. explained that after graduation, the two best qualifiers at the rifle range (those were the two highest scorers) would get the steam irons. The Marine Corps is very, very picky about qualifying with their weapon, which was then the M-1. We spent three weeks at the rifle range, like all the other recruits, snapping in and firing, with qualification the last day of the three-week period. At that time, you shot the last ten rounds at a 500-yard target, which is a long way. Anyway, to make a long story short, <u>I won the steam iron</u>. It was a mixed blessing because from there on to graduation, the D.I. knew my name. Up to then, I had tried not to rock any boats.

After graduation, I went to the PX and saw something that sort of startled me. There on the counter was the exact same steam iron that I had won, for about $10 or $12! And I figured the D.I. must have got really confused when he paid $300 for two steam irons! (Unless, of course, he kept the change.) I remember another time when we "bought him" four new tires for his car so he could go on liberty one weekend.

South Camp Fuji

After Boot Camp at Parris Island, and then Marine combat training at Camp Geiger, I was an M.P. at the Camp Lejeune main gate in North Carolina. I was finally sent to Japan where I spent a tour of 14 months at South Camp Fuji. At that time, South Camp Fuji might have been the most dangerous assignment in the whole Marine Corps. Right outside our main gate and the barbed wire fence surrounding our camp was the small town of Fujioka. This town had probably 90-plus bars. Each bar had "hostesses," and venereal disease ran rampant. It was a very dangerous place to be stationed. Of course, I spent most of my free time at the camp library. It was at this library that I mastered my vocabulary and command of the English language. That library certainly contributed to me being so articulate today.

In Uniform on a Japanese Train

When I had weekend liberty, I would go to Tokyo or some of the rest and relaxation (what we called "R&R") hotels taken over by the Army after World War II. One weekend, I'd gone to an R&R hotel in downtown Tokyo called the Rocker-Four Club. Coming back, I got on the train going to Gotimba when I realized that everyone on the car was missing a limb. The passengers that were amputees were looking at me. Finally, I figured out that they were all former soldiers of the Japanese army who had been badly wounded and lost a limb in the war. They were probably in a veteran's hospital that had taken them to Tokyo for the weekend. They really didn't like Marines, and I was in my Marine uniform. I was a little uncomfortable.

In Uniform with a Dead Man

Duty in Japan was training and more training, including an amphibious landing on Okinawa. When I was on liberty at Tokyo, which was still bombed out in many places, I stumbled on a disheveled old Japanese man lying on a bench. I thought he might have been dead. Many of the NCOs in our company were in the islands fighting against the Japanese during World War II, and a lot of them had stories to tell about killing Japanese soldiers. I really wanted my picture taken with a dead Japanese. I sat down next to the man and had my buddy take my picture of me with my arm sort of around him. It plainly shows I was a Marine sitting with a dead Japanese man.

The POW at South Camp Fuji

One of my fellow Marines was Technical Sergeant

Corky Thayer. Corky had been captured by the Japanese at Wake, early in the war. When he was captured, Corky was a private. When he got out of prison, he was a gunnery sergeant. It was the practice then for our POWs to get the next grade in rank after they had served the minimum time in the previous grade. While he was in POW camp, Corky had gone from private to gunnery sergeant. He had spent most of the war at South Camp Fuji, where we were now stationed, as it was then a POW camp. Corky knew most of the Japanese civilian workers. For instance, the barber had been one of his guards. He knew the people that maintained the outside of the buildings and grounds who were just day laborers. He knew all of them. They had either worked at the prison camp or had been guards. He would talk to them, and he had a great command of the Japanese language, as you might imagine. What was really interesting was that he seemed to bear no hate or resentment.

Captain Norfolk and the Inspection

One night there was a tremendous fire in Fujioka. The buildings and all the bars were built with rice straw and were very inflammable. The next morning, we fell out, and our company commander (Captain Ira P. Norfolk) addressed us. It seems that the fire was set deliberately. Someone from my outfit—Charlie Company, First Batt, Third Marines—was a suspect.

That morning, the army CID (Criminal Investigation Department), along with Marine investigators, wanted a couple of girls to walk through our ranks and pick out the culprit who set the town on fire. Our company commander, Ira P. Norfolk, refused to let that happen. A little later, there was a big conference with Captain Norfolk, the CID, and the Marine Corps Battalion Commander. They won the argument. We fell out and opened ranks, and the CID officer and the hostess from one of the bars walked through, looking at each one of the men in our company. She finally stopped in front of one person and pointed. We never saw that Marine again. Prior to letting them walk through our ranks, Captain Norfolk gave a speech that I've never forgotten. He said, "Gentlemen, in the proud history of the United States Marine Corps since its inception, at Tuns Tavern to the halls of Montezuma to the shores of Tripoli, this is the first time that a Marine Corps company has been inspected by a whore!" He did not like that situation whatsoever.

I'm sure the CID guys didn't like him. Captain Norfolk had fought the Japanese through the islands, which probably influenced his feelings about the matter. After all, only 30 or 40 buildings were burned down and nobody got hurt. Big deal.

Ira P. Norfolk, as I said, was our company commander. I wanted to name our first child Ira P. Early, but I was overruled because his initials would have been "I. P. Early," so I named him Patrick instead.

Proud to Be a Marine

In December of 1955, I was promoted to sergeant and got to move into the sergeant's quarters where I had a Japanese house-boy. (No more polishing shoes and ironing uniforms for this old Marine.)

I loved the Marine Corps. The men I served with in Charlie Company were like brothers. Bud Black, Walt Cope,

Big Davis, Little Davis, and others. The Marine Corps is all about team work. You never let your fellow Marines down.

We lived together; we got in fights together. I was closer to them than any brother (even though I was an only child and didn't have a brother). I thought I would never forget them, but here 50-plus years later, I only remember the names of a few.

Were those guys in my company as tough as today's great Marines? I think probably so. Many of my pals never finished high school. Most of them were from the southern states. But they were good men, and those that stayed in for 20 years and fought in Vietnam were as good as anybody who served before or after. They were gung-ho Marines.

I have always considered the title "Marine" an honor. It has been 50-plus years since my D.I. pinned on my collar the Eagle, Globe, and Anchor at Parris Island, South Carolina. It is still the proudest moment of my life.

Chapter 3
Early Politics 101

I married my wife, Barbara, while I was in the Marine Corps. I had gotten her a "political job" with the Knox County Treasurer. She had saved enough from her allotment money and her job to buy a 24 x 8-foot house trailer. We parked it in Vincennes with the T and T crowd. (That's "trailers and tattoos.")

After I was discharged, I got a job with the state Highway Department cutting weeds with a briar scythe along Highway 50 between Vincennes and Washington. Some really big snakes were along that road, as well as mammoth, champion chiggers. Some of those chiggers were as big as house flies. I wanted to enter one as a State Fair exhibit, but they didn't have that category.

A Bridge, Limb Lines, a Catfish, and the Superintendent

The next summer, I got promoted. I ran an air hammer, and I painted bridges. One bridge I painted was on a road between Highway 41 and Decker. The bridge was over the Dischee Creek, almost to White River. It was good catfishing. I had a good idea that I could paint the bridge and watch some limb lines I set out for catfish. My idea worked, and I had caught several. As luck would have it, I was painting away, and the District Superintendent drove up to see how my painting was coming along. He climbed out of his car to talk to me, and I noticed a limb line going crazy just a short distance from the bridge. Luckily, his back was turned because a big cat had hooked himself and was bending a good-sized limb down in the water, and it was splashing. I was glad when he left as I wasn't sure he would approve of my limb lines. I would have hated to lose such a great job.

When the fall came, we moved to Bloomington, and I enrolled in the School of Business at Indiana University. We had the GI Bill stipend of $130 per month and also soon had our first child, our son Pat (not Ira P., but Pat). I joined the Young Republicans Club. A couple of the officers at that time were Richard Bray from Martinsville (now a state senator) and Carl Van Doren from Kokomo, who later was the Circuit Court Judge.

We still lived in our 24-foot house trailer. We had a dog in those days, and we were really poor. Our dog had only three legs. We called him Tripod. It was sort of fun to watch him with only one back leg trying to pee. In fact, the neighbors would come over to watch.

I know this is hard to believe, but I graduated with honors from Indiana University. I was inducted in both the business honorary Beta Gamma Sigma and the accounting honorary Beta Alpha Psi. And when I graduated, I had more ropes and ribbons on my gown than some Argentine admiral. My family was very proud. And I never did have to take algebra or calculus.

I graduated from IU with a degree from the business school, and a major in accounting. After a few Big Eight accounting firm interviews, I decided I would rather have a dead rat in my mouth than work for a Big Eight firm as an accountant. The placement bureau at the IU School of Business was really good. Graduating with honors and having already been in the military and having a family was a plus. I had lots of interviews, and I was offered a job with almost every interview—except IBM. Their milk-toast interviewer didn't like my Marine Corps haircut. I wasn't IBM material, I guess. I've always hated IBM since then, and I hope its stock keeps going down.

A Bigger Fish in a Smaller Pond

Besides the campus interviews, the placement people had a book of job opportunities from small firms. These firms didn't come on campus, but they had an opening or were looking for an IU School of Business graduate. Well, that was for me. I became interested in one of those job opportunities. It was with an Indianapolis consulting engineering firm that wanted a business manager who would handle all the administrative duties. Sounded good to me. I'd be a bigger fish in a smaller pond. And besides that, they were offering $100 per week, and most of the others were offering $4,800 per year. I took the job, and I felt I did the right thing. They even gave me an old used car to drive. Here I was making a hundred a week with a car. And soon, I was a Republican Precinct Committeeman who lived in the upstairs of a furnished duplex. I was shitting in tall cotton.

The couch in that duplex was a little suspect. Upon moving in, my wife found a great big dog bone under the cushions. That upstairs duplex I had rented was in the 600 block of Gray Street. (Don't go there today!)

New Precinct Commiteeman

I immediately went to the Marion County Courthouse to register to vote for the next election. The lady who registered me to vote introduced herself as Ruth Marshall. She was the 9th Ward Chairman. I had just moved into her ward. When I identified myself as a Republican, she asked whether I would like to be a Precinct Committeeman in the 5th Precinct, which is where I had just moved. According to her, the person who had been the Precinct Committeeman there had just gone to jail, and I answered "Sure, I'll do it." So began my start in Marion County politics.

A New Ward Chairman

A year later, H. Dale Brown, the County Chairman, had a falling out with Ruth Marshall and fired her as the 9th Ward Chairman. Dale called an old war-horse, Maudie Smith, who had been the county vice-chairman many years before and was now one of the 9th Ward Committeemen. Dale asked her to replace Ruth Marshall. She said because of her age, she would take the Ward Vice-chairman if Dale would appoint Rex Early as the Ward Chairman. Dale said okay and appointed me, as probably the youngest Ward Chairman that he had ever appointed. That was in 1959.

The Politics of Engineering

It was about this time I made an interesting discovery. As Precinct Committeeman and Ward Chairman, I got to know some of our Republican officeholders, including the Republican County Commissioners. They were the same county commissioners who gave out engineering contracts. The engineering contracts, of course, were professional services and not bid. Besides being the administrator of our company, I became the "business-getter."(Oh what a great discovery!)

After about 18 months with the firm, three of the engineers wanted to break off to start their own firm and wanted me to go along as a full partner. Early in 1960, we formed Mid-States Engineering Corporation. We had one contract: a subdivision in Kokomo called Indian Heights. I went 48 weeks without a paycheck. I think I had borrowed as much as I could from my father-in-law and from one of my partners.

Things then started to turn around, and we started having a little cash flow. Then we started getting some meaningful contracts from the county, as well as a big contract from the city. Even though we had a Democrat mayor, I became friends with the Director of Public Works, a great guy named Elsworth Maxwell, who gave us some contracts because he thought we did good work.

Rex Gave a Client's Apartment to the City

One of our clients was The Lusk Corporation. They were land developers. They developed one of the first Section 8 projects in Indianapolis, on Shadeland Avenue.

The project's streets were built to city specifications. It came time to dedicate the streets to the city. Our company wrote the metes and bounds legal description of the street that was to be dedicated. The legal document for dedication set out the description of the property owned by the developer, and then stated that the owner of the described property would dedicate to the city the following described real estate (the description of the roads).

Pretty simple, huh? Except that my secretary got the legal descriptions mixed up, and we kept the streets and gave the project to the city.

Stan Telesnick, the Democrat City Attorney, and Elsworth Maxwell, the Democrat head of the Board of Works, called me to thank me for the gift. They said the income would sure help the city's budget.

They must have thought that I had a room-temperature IQ because I told them to "get off my street."

They were good guys and helped this Republican more than once.

The Loud Collections Guy

When we opened our company doors, our main customers were builders and developers who hadn't paid the engineering and surveying firm they had used before.

Keeping cash flow was somewhat a problem, and it was my problem. We had a milk-toast attorney whose office was next door. My office and his office were separated by a thin wall. One day, he asked my partner whether I made collection calls on any specific day. It seems that he had an elderly client in his office one day when I was yelling, cursing, and threatening one of our clients who would not pay his bill. He didn't want any of his clients in his office while I was trying to collect money from slow payers.

Engineering Success

I stayed at Mid-States Engineering for 22 years, from 1960 until 1982. Through the years, Sol Miller and I bought out the other two partners, leaving Sol and me fifty-fifty partners. We designed subdivisions, shopping centers, sewers, and highways. Also, we had survey crews, an airplane, and a photo lab, with which we did aerial photography and surveying.

In the late '80s and early '90s, my partner, Sol, had the vision to get us into aerial surveying and computer-driven digitizing for utilities and the federal government. (I never really understood how it worked.) It was a great success.

Engineering and Campaigns

About that time, we had a buy-out offer from a large firm. I was tired of doing the same old thing, and besides that, our engineering competitors had finally woke up and started playing the political card. I felt that some of their campaign contributions were obscene and would eventually lead to trouble, but obviously never has. Engineering firms yet today are probably the biggest contributors to mayors, governors, and county commissioners. You won't believe what they give to both parties and their candidates. I would work in the political arena, but I wasn't about to get into the "who could give the most money" race and buy businesses. Look at contributions to the former mayor of Indianapolis, Indiana, Bart Peterson. How much came from engineers?

I was ready to sell out. In the meantime, our firm slowly shifted from engineering design to computerized mapping. Sol, my partner, didn't want to sell, so in 1982, he bought me out. My 50 percent went to Sol. When I left, we had about 130 employees. It had grown really too big for me. And after I was gone, Mid-States Engineering had as many 300 employees. Sol and I were partners for 22 years and never had a disagreement. I think it's because he knew I was always right.

Chapter 4
The Dale Brown Era

Dale Brown was the last of the old-time political bosses. He was the master of grass-roots politics and he ruled with patronage and fear. The fear part was that you were probably going to lose your patronage job if you crossed him. I actually heard him pick up the phone and tell one of our Supreme Court Judges how to rule on a certain issue. He knew every Precinct Committeeman and Ward Chairman by name. He rewarded his friends and never forgot his enemies.

When Dale was the Marion County Republican Chairman, every precinct was polled. That meant that a volunteer (usually the committeeman) would knock on every door, determine who lived there, and got the unregistered Republicans registered. Patronage workers were expected to help. In order to get a patronage job in the city, county, or state, you had to get the Republican Precinct Committeeman and Ward Chairman to sign off on your application. The job seeker would also agree to give 2 percent of his take-home pay to the party. Dale had a "collector" in each office. Even the judges paid their 2 percent, as well as the other Republican office holders.

In 1959, Dale appointed me 9th Ward Chairman. I worked hard and was a good Ward Chairman. Dale liked me. At one of the State Conventions, he asked me to stay close, and on several occasions, he told me I would be his successor, which was a job I didn't want. In 1963, prior to Unigov, (the consolidation of the City of Indianapolis and Marion County), Dale appointed me as City Chairman to help manage the Republican candidate for the mayoral campaign. Dale had gotten me slated, nominated, and elected to the State Legislature in 1962. He was good to me.

The Indianapolis Star did not like Dale. He had risen to the top of the Marion County Republican party in 1952. Just about every Indiana Republican was for Robert Taft for President in the upcoming convention. Dale was for Eisenhower.

Indiana, Taft,
and the Republican National Convention

At the 1952 National Convention, Cale Holder (who would later be a federal judge) was state chairman, and Bill Jenner (a United States Senator) led the Indiana charge for Taft. Taft got every Indiana vote but three. Eugene Pulliam, owner of The Star, was one of the three. The rest were for Taft. The vote was taken, and Ike won the nomination. As was the practice after the vote was counted and a winner established, the Chair would call another roll call of the states, and every state would make it unanimous. They didn't know Indiana very well. When Indiana's Cale Holder and Bill Jenner were called upon, Cale got up and responded, "We're still for our man, Taft!" As you might well imagine, this caused quite an uproar at the National Convention. I loved Bill Jenner and Cale Holder.

The Brown Faithful Rewards

In 1952, Dale Brown, the County Clerk, was the big winner. He had been a strong Eisenhower supporter. At the same time, George Craig was running for governor, and Dale threw his support behind Craig, which meant that Dale not only had control of the federal patronage but a lot of influence as far as state patronage was concerned. This meant jobs and contracts for the Brown faithful. Besides patronage jobs that Dale handed out, there were other types of patronage for his soldiers.

APPRAISALS

Most of the time when the city or state had a construction project, a right of way was bought. The procedure was this: The state or city appraisers gave the property owner a price they would pay for the right of way. If this property owner wasn't satisfied with the price, he took the case to court. Our judges would then appoint three citizens to make an independent appraisal. The appointments were always one certified, card-carrying appraiser, and the other two citizens always turned out to be Ward Chairmen or Precinct Committeemen. Almost all the bailiffs were Ward Chairmen, and it sure was nice when they called you to come over to the court and get sworn in as an appraiser. We met in court, set a time to look at the property, and then usually agreed with the professional appraiser. The fees ran from $200–$500. I had a bunch of them.

The Repair Shop Payback

On one occasion, I was appointed to appraise a piece of property that had a small repair shop. A couple of years earlier, I had taken something there to get repaired, and I got charged more for the repair than I had paid for the item. Despite that injustice, I really tried to be fair, but I did feel that our professional appraiser had over-valued the property to be taken. I expressed myself, and he agreed. Actually, as I remember, we appraised the property for less than the state had offered. (Paybacks are hell.)

RECEIVERSHIPS

Much like the appraisals, the courts had business receiverships filed in the courts. If, in fact, a business was put into receivership, a receiver had to be appointed to close the business and sell the assets. Guess who most of those receivers were? You guessed it: Republican Ward Chairmen and Committeemen. (Sometimes some of the judges' buddies would slip in.)

The Receiver and the Suspect

I was appointed receiver of an engine-exchange business. They rebuilt and sold used car and truck engines. The Honorable Chuck Daughtery appointed me. I posted bond, called a locksmith, and drove to the property.

When I got there, a truck was pulled into the building, and there were two or three people loading the assets on the trucks. I identified myself as the court-appointed receiver and asked what in the hell were they doing. The owner spoke up and said if I didn't get out of his building, he would kill me. Now I was young and sort of stupid, so we got into a cussing fight. I explained to him that Judge Daughtery would really be upset if he killed me. He finally packed up and left. Later, I recognized him as being the prime suspect in the famous LaSalle Street murders. He was never convicted, and the case was never solved. I'm glad he didn't kill me.

I sold off the stuff and received a fee from the court. Like the appraisals, the Dale Brown organization got most of the receiverships. I got my share, too.

The Arrest of Dale Brown

Now Dale still had his enemies. Alex Clark was the Mayor of Indianapolis. At one time, he was also the Marion County Republican Chairman. Alex Clark did not get along with Dale Brown. One evening, Alex got a call at home to inform him that Dale Brown was at the Columbia Club, and he had way too much to drink. Alex called his Police Chief, who stationed a policeman at all four of the Monument Circle exits. Sure enough, Dale, whose car was parked in front of the club, came out, jumped in his car, and started home.

He was immediately arrested and charged with driving while intoxicated. Dale pled not guilty. Come the day of the trial before the Honorable Scott McDonald, who was a staunch Republican, Dale stood before the bench.

The Trial of Dale Brown

The Deputy Prosecutor was a real young attorney named Keith Bulen. He presented the evidence, and when he was finished, Judge McDonald asked him. "Are you the prosecutor or the defense attorney?"

The prosecutor's case was so bad, Judge McDonald had no choice but to find Dale Brown not guilty. You don't suppose an ambitious young man took the tank, do you?

Not long after that, Keith Bulen was appointed as the Marion County Young Republican Chairman. He was appointed by Dale Brown.

Now I might have been appointed 9th Ward Chairman in the Dale Brown era, but it was an old political war-horse named Maude Smith who got me appointed. Dale had gotten into a bitter fight with Ruth Marshall and had fired her as the 9th Ward Chairman. (Ruth Marshall was the lady who first registered me in 1958.)

Dale had asked Maude to take her place, and Maude (being up in years) told Dale she would be the Ward Vice-chairman if he would appoint Rex Early as the Ward Chairman so I could do the work.

The 9th Ward was from Oakland on the west, Michigan on the South, Emerson on the east, and the railroad tracks on the North. We had 18 precincts. I was also the precinct committeeman of the 5th precinct. The Dearborn Hotel was in my precinct.

Maude had been the County Vice-chairman back in the '30's or early '40's. She was a widow lady with no children and had always held a political job as one of the court's deputy clerks.

The Name with No Lever

After Dale had appointed me as a Ward Chairman, he asked me to find someone to beat Ruth Marshall as precinct committeeperson.

His thought was to keep her busy on Election Day in her own precinct so she wouldn't be out in the ward trying to beat Dale's slate.

Finding someone in her precinct to run against her was

an impossible task. She was loved by all (except Dale). Finally, I found someone. His name was Carl, and he worked at the Republican State Headquarters as a go-fer (go-fer this, go-fer that). Of course, Carl did not want to run against Mrs. Marshall. But after a little arm twisting and a job threat, Carl came around. Now Carl was a little fellow. It is not politically correct to call him a midget; he was vertically impaired.

On Election Day, as the 9th Ward Chairman, I started making my rounds of the Ward about 9 in the morning. Carl reported that everything was going fine. I made another round about 2 p.m., and again Carl reported that everything was going fine. My final round was at 5 p.m. with the polls closing at 6 p.m.. This time, Carl was upset as he had just gone into the voting machine and found that the little lever above his name was missing. Someone, somehow, had probably inserted a screwdriver behind his lever and popped the lever off. I asked Carl, "What did you do when you found you couldn't vote for yourself?" Carl said, "I just voted for that nice Mrs. Marshall." Carl got no votes that day. Dale wasn't very happy with me.

The Making of a Legislator

Starting in 1961, Maude Smith started insisting that I run for the state legislature. I tried to explain that for one thing, I had started my business (Mid-States Engineering) in 1960, and we were still small and struggling. Also, I was the father of two small children and would soon have three. And most importantly, Marion County had 11 house seats, and all 11 were Republicans. There were no openings. But Maude would not take no for an answer.

Early in 1962, Maude called me to her house. She again started her legislature lecture and went one step farther. She got on the telephone and made an appointment for me with one of her old friends. I heard the conversation. She said, "Joe, I want you to get my friend Rex Early in the legislature. I know you don't fool with that stuff anymore, but I also know you can do it. Joe, I don't care what you say. I'm sending this young man down to your office this afternoon, and I expect you to take care of it." Or words to that effect.

She said I needed to get into a suit. The only suit I had was a JCPenney special with sweat rings under the arms that the cleaners couldn't get out. I could wear it in both the summer and the winter.

I went as instructed and was embarrassed as I went downtown to a law firm and announced I had an appointment with Joe. I was ushered into a big office, and there behind an enormous desk was a small, elderly man. He asked me a few questions, like, "Why in the hell would you want to be in the legislature?" Then he laughed about Maude Smith's insistence on him helping me. Joe finally picked up the telephone and called Dale Brown, the County Chair, and told Dale he wanted me in the legislature. I am sure Dale told him we already had a full contingent, but Joe was pretty insistent.

Later, Dale called me and asked whether I would run and told me I had his support, and support me he did. I was slated, nominated, and elected, along with 10 other Republicans from Marion County.

I was very impressed at what Joe Daniels, the senior partner in Baker and Daniels, could get done. One phone call from Maude Smith, and Dale Brown dropped an incumbent Republican and supported me. Mr. Daniels had been the Republican District Chairman in the 1940s when Jim Bradford (Judge Cale Bradford's grandfather) had been County Chairman.

Indiana's Battle of the Budget

In the 1963 session, the House had a large Republican majority. The Senate, however, had a one- or two-vote Republican majority. One of the Republican senators died during the session, which created a real problem. Even though Governor Welch was a Democrat, the Lt. Governor (Dick Ristine, from Crawfordsville) was a Republican.

The state, as usual, was broke, and it was obvious that taxes were going to be increased. The Republican leadership in the House, with the support of the Senate, wanted a sales tax and an adjusted gross income tax. The Democrats, led by Governor Welch, and Bob Rock (the Democrat minority leader) were dead-set against a sales tax and wanted more income tax.

The session got down to the end, and there was no compromising. Keith Bulen, our Marion County Leader of our 11 House members, had joined the Ristine/House leadership plan of a new sales tax.

Jim Clark, Dave Caldwell, Star Brown, and I felt that a Democrat governor had spent the money, and thus it was up to him and the Democrats to raise taxes, not the Republicans. The House, as well as our Marion County delegation, was torn apart. Tempers flared in our caucus, and people were changing their minds and waffling on an hourly basis.

The leadership pointed out that the one constitutional duty the House had to fulfill was to pass the budget. The budget bill came down, and all the Democrats voted against it. They said it was not enough money. A handful of Republicans voted against it, including Clark, Caldwell, Brown, and myself, saying it was too much money—and lo and behold, we beat the budget. Soon after that, with no chance of compromise, the session ended with no budget, and Governor Welch immediately called a 40-day Special Session.

After the vote on the budget, tempers were flaring, and a lot of finger-pointing was going on. John Coppes, the Chairman of the Ways and Means Committee from Nappanee, got in my face and vowed he would never again vote for any Marion County bill. I assured him that I didn't give a "red rat's butt" how he voted. The argument became a little more intense, and there was a little shoving (no blows, just shoving). Finally Representative Dunbar from Osgood, a great big man, stepped between us.

During the special session, the Democrats and the majority of the Republicans passed a budget as well as the sales tax and the gross income tax. This, much to my chagrin, was labeled as a "Republican bill and a Republican tax increase." They even maneuvered the vote in the Senate, where Dick Ristine (the Lt. Governor and the leading candidate to be the Republican nominee for governor) had to cast the deciding vote. We also had passed a "wheel tax" for Marion County. The public was pissed.

Early Departure from the Legislature

In 1964, the Marion County Republicans supported Bill Bray for Governor. However, Lt. Governor Dick Ristine, despite a spirited battle at the State Convention, won the Republican nomination for governor. He was labeled as a tax raiser and lost by a large margin. In all deference to Dick Ristine, 1964 was a disaster for Republicans all over the country with Lyndon B. Johnson beating Barry Goldwater badly.

I was born at night, but not last night, and I realized that when Republicans raised taxes, we were going to get beat in 1964. So I didn't run along with Bulen and several others. I was right; all 11 of the Republican legislative candidates got beat soundly. I figured that was coming. It wasn't my first rodeo. There were other reasons I didn't run; a growing family, the 40-day Special Session that didn't go over well with my business partners, and pay of only $1,800 per year.

My legislative career was not without some highlights. The Cold War was going full blast, and Castro and the Communists had taken over Cuba. It looked like any day, we and Russia could start dropping bombs. You get the picture.

Polish Hams and the License That Wasn't

Well I found out that Standard Grocery was selling Polish hams. Poland then was a Communist country. I proposed a law that anyone selling goods from a Communist country had to have a state license. My bill stated that the license must be 3 x 5-foot and displayed where it could be seen. The license, in bold letters, would read, "THIS ESTABLISHMENT IS LICENSED TO SELL COMMUNIST GOODS." My bill never got a hearing.

The Liberty Amendment

Dale Brown called me one day and asked whether I would sponsor an amendment to the United States

Constitution. Herman Krannert, of Inland Container (a big Republican contributor) called Dale and was interested in the Liberty Amendment. Basically, if it passed, this amendment would considerably limit the federal government from providing anything but basic services. The federal government could provide us only with national defense (Army, Navy, Marines, and Air Force), build the interstate highway system, and a few other things. They could not delve into education, health care plans, Social Security, etc. Only the states and local governments could provide these types of services.

There was an ongoing effort all over the country by states to pass the Liberty Amendment. It was so conservative it would have made Rush Limbaugh's philosophy look like a form of socialism.

I introduced the bill, and it was assigned to a committee who gave it a hearing. The Star gave the bill a lot of ink. When it came time for the House Committee hearing, literally 1,000 people showed up. Ninety percent were conservatives who supported this bill.

The plan was that a spokesman from Texas would speak for the bill at the committee hearing, and another spokesman would speak in opposition. Loudspeakers were set up in the rotunda and outside on the State House lawn even though this was an evening hearing around March, and it was cold outside. The crowd was boisterous and loud and was a sight to behold. Don Tabbert, a local conservative attorney, helped me write my opening remarks.

The amendment passed out of the House Committee and got to the floor. The vote was 50 in favor and 49 opposed. In announcing the vote, Dick Guthrie, a Marion County

Republican, stated that the Speaker votes yes. So, the bill passed the House with 51 votes.

Wendell Martin, a great Republican State Senator, carried the bill in the Senate. The bill passed out to the floor and was beaten by two votes. Jack Ruckelshaus and Robert Brokenbur, both from Marion County, voted no. Other than money bills, this was the most controversial bill in the legislature. It was fun being the sponsor. The Liberty Amendment was never passed by any state.

The Christmas Party Ended Quickly

In December of 1963, Dale Brown called and asked whether I wanted to have a Christmas party for my Precinct Committee and Vice-committeemen. Dale said he would pay for it. I was making $150 per week. We chose a family restaurant out on East Washington Street, Bradley's Bar-B-Q. It had a private party room, was reasonably priced, and had great chicken that was cheap.

Come the big night, and all the players were there, including Dale and Mary Brown. The only person missing was our County Vice Chairman. Now our new Vice Chairman was a lovely lady although on the portly side; actually, she was short and fat. She always wore a black dress. Most of the time, it had accumulated face powder and whatever else she might have spilled on it, but she was nice.

After a social hour, the restaurant owner came to me and said, "The chicken is ready." I asked him to wait until our Vice Chairman arrived. After a wait, the owner said, "The chicken is going to get cold." I said to go ahead and serve it. We were about half-way through the meal when the missing guests showed up, huffing and puffing and apologetic. Our

Vice Chairman's husband was as small of stature as she was large. He announced, "I'm sorry we are late, folks, but I had to give Mama an enema." It was really more information than we needed, especially during dinner. I did get credit on my bill because very few ordered desert. (I know that's crude, but it's the truth.)

Two and Sixteen Votes

As time went on, Dale Brown's political organization started falling apart. We had not elected a Republican mayor since 1951. We took a bad beating in 1964, and the troops were getting restless.

About 1965, Dale began to get paranoid. He would start every Ward Chairmen's meeting with a roll call. He would then ask each Ward Chairman about his (Dale's) support for another term as County Chairman. He started at the 1st Ward and work down. Most of the Ward Chairmen, to escape Dale's wrath, said. "One-hundred percent of the Precinct Committeemen are for you." He came to the 9th Ward, my ward. I said, "Two and 16." He was mad. "Who are the two against me?" he asked. I said, "No, Dale. It's two for you." He went berserk, yelling at me. I shot back. "Dale, I'm one of the two for you. Don't yell at me!"

Chapter 5
Bulen Days

Keith Bulen was a great politician. He recruited a cadre of young, energetic, smart people, and they loved him. Dale Brown's organization had gotten old and tired. Keith had new committeemen and Ward Chairmen everywhere.

Keith's first year as County Chairman, 1966, was a Republican year. Keith turned it around. We elected 11 Republican house members and five senators as well as the county offices. When Keith got elected, he asked me back in the fold as an assistant County Chairman. There were no hard feelings. He knew I would be loyal to Dale Brown to the last, but I had one strike against me. The 1967 election turned out to be the most important election this city ever had. It was time to elect a mayor. The candidates were Bill Sharp (who later became a judge); former mayor and war hero, Alex Clark; and an Indianapolis Public Schools (IPS) board member, Dick Lugar. Alex Clark was a bona fide hero. He was decorated with the Silver Star and Purple Heart, to name a few of his awards.

The Screening for Indianapolis Mayor

Keith appointed a "screening committee" to pick our candidate. John Burkhart was named chairman.

Keith sent out a questionnaire on Marion County Republican stationery to every Committeeman, Vice Committeeman, Ward and Vice Ward Chairmen, plus contributors and others to see who they felt would have the best chance to win the Mayoral race: Clark, Lugar, or Sharp. I was strong for Alex Clark. He was my mentor, hero, and pal.

One day, while in headquarters, I "borrowed" several reams of paper of Keith's letterhead and several boxes of his envelopes. After all, they had plenty. After reproducing the questionnaire on the appropriate letterhead, we had a marking party. We sent back hundreds of the questionnaires, all marked for our man, Alex Clark.

During the slating process, I repeatedly asked John Burkhart what the questionnaires recommended. Mr. Burkhart would not tell me. He said they were inconclusive. I bet! I asked him for the questionnaire so many times, I think he smelled a rat.

Keith appointed approximately 20 people on the screening committee. Keith tried to be fair. He appointed me to represent Alex Clark, John Sweezy to represent Bill Sharp, and the other 18 to represent Dick Lugar. (Keith took no chances.)

This 1967 screening committee interviewed all three candidates plus a young minister who wanted to run for something, named Bill Hudnut. The screening committee voted, and as Gomer Pyle used to say, "Surprise, surprise, surprise!" Dick Lugar won the screening.

The results were hushed up until that evening when

Keith called a Ward Chairman's meeting. When Keith announced that it was Lugar, pandemonium broke out. The Ward Chairman knew next to nothing about Dick Lugar. A few knew he had been on the IPS board where he had voted for busing. This disturbed some people. Many knew Dick's mother, Bertha Lugar, who had been in the political arena in the Dale Brown days. She was a wonderful woman, and everyone liked Bertha.

After some blistering remarks by some of the Ward Chairman, Keith and his leadership quieted everyone down.

Unslated Mayoral Candidate

Prior to 1967, Alex Clark was the last Republican mayor of Indianapolis, elected in 1951 and serving one four-year term. Besides being a war hero, he was loved by just about everyone, from the Woodstock's Country Club silk-stockings to the hully-gullys in Mars Hill. Those that knew Alex liked him.

When Alex didn't get slated, a couple of things happened. Alex felt the fix was in at the screening (and it was), and lots of Alex's old friends urged him to run, slated or not slated.

Alex decided to run. He asked P.K. Ward, a well-known attorney, and yours truly to be his campaign managers. We had only three months before the election, and Keith had already recruited a great organization. They all loved Keith and saw this as a new beginning for the Republican Party. I truly believe, and with no disrespect to Dick Lugar, that Keith could have gotten Benito Mussolini elected in that primary. The Republican voters saw Bulen and his organization as having new ideas versus the old guard, and they wanted a change.

The Republican Fight Begins

That spring campaign was hard fought with charges and counter-charges flying in every direction. Bill Sharp, the other candidate, passed up by the screening committee, endorsed Clark as did Don Tabbert and his conservative following.

Lugar proved himself to be a hard worker and a fast learner. He jumped head-long into the fray where more timid souls would have asked, "Bulen, what did you get me into?" Wards met practically every night. Some meetings were very friendly to Dick Lugar's candidacy; others were not so friendly. He was a lot tougher than we thought, and he didn't melt.

As I said before, this election was the most significant election that I have ever experienced. Ironically, the Democrats decided that they would have a big primary fight. As it turned out, THEIR FIGHT RESULTED IN THE REPUBLICANS HOLDING THE MAYOR'S OFFICE FOR 32 CONSECUTIVE YEARS.

The Republican primary was pretty hard fought, but it was nothing compared to the rancor of the Democrat fight.
The Democrat Rancor: Old Guard versus Young Turks

The Democrat County Chairman was Jim Beatty, a respected lawyer, who had decided he would take on his incumbent Democrat, Mayor John Barton. Mayor Barton was a laid-back, kind, Irish politician. Jim Beatty headed up a group of young, aggressive Democrats, several of whom were elected to the Legislature in 1964 and called themselves The Young Turks. These young guys wanted to take over the party from the "old guys." So the Democrat County Chairman, Beatty, ran against the incumbent mayor.

Why a County Chairman would run against his incumbent mayor is anybody's guess. The Democrats' fight in that primary was something! Our Republican primary fight got pretty wild, but it was like a walk in the park when compared with the Democrat fight.

After all the smoke cleared, John Barton, the Democrat mayor, won the primary. And Dick Lugar, the new guy on the block, won the Republican primary.

Jim Morris Meets Richard Lugar

During the campaign, I got a call from Frank McKinney, Sr., president of American Fletcher National Bank. He was a former Democrat National Chairman under President Harry Truman. Also, he was a friend of Alex Clark, and was Murray Clark's grandfather.

Mr. McKinney asked how I was fixed on manpower. Any campaign needs manpower. He sent me two newly hired trainees at the bank. One was named Jim Morris. We put Jim as the head of our Young Republicans for Clark and gave him various duties in the Clark campaign. Jim Morris loved politics, and he had worked on a congressional campaign while he was at Indiana University.

Jim, like all of us, was devastated that Alex had lost. A few days after the primary, Jim called me and explained that Lugar needed a driver for his campaign and that the bank told Jim that he could finish out the campaign. Jim was a little concerned that if he took the job, he would be looked upon as being "unfaithful" to Alex. My advice was hey, the primary was over, and Dick Lugar was our candidate. Go for it. Jim did and forged a great friendship with Dick, who recognized that Jim was one smart dude.

Jim has been Deputy Mayor (under Lugar), president of Lilly Endowment when they helped build the Hoosier Dome, Chairman of the Board of Trustees of Indiana State University, Chairman of the Board of Trustees of Indiana University, president of the Indianapolis Water Company, Member of the U.S. Olympic Committee, major player in the Pan Am Games, head of the World Food Bank, and Rex Early's assistant in the Alex Clark campaign. Jim's accomplishments have been both incredible and remarkable (Jim's two favorite words). I just know he is especially proud of being my assistant in the Clark campaign. That obviously helped him get some of his big jobs. How could you beat that resume? Even though Jim was MIA (missing in action) during my governor's campaign, we have remained friends, and I admire his successes.

The Judge and His Bow Tie

As the primary battle was being fought every day, there were rumors that the Democrat County Chairman and the Republican County Chairman had some kind of a deal. The Alex Clark people filed a lawsuit that accused the Jim Beatty Democrats and the Keith Bulen Republicans of having a sweetheart contract: that Bulen was helping Beatty, and Beatty was helping Lugar.

I was in court the day the lawsuit was first heard by the honorable Judge Rufus Kuykendall. The Clark force's logo was a blue, polka dot bow tie. Alex Clark always wore a blue, polka dot bow tie. The campaign gave out actual ties as well as badges shaped and colored like the ties.

When the judge came in and the bailiff called the court to order, the bailiff stopped and whispered to the judge, who then removed his blue, polka dot tie. Needless to say, we liked the judge. I think the case was continued until after the primary election, when it became moot. We just filed the lawsuit for the publicity.

Republicans Unite with Chicken and Beer

With the primary over, it was time for the party to get geared up for the fall election. Now the demographics of the "old city" of Indianapolis made it near impossible to elect a Republican for mayor. Even with Bulen's magic and a candidate like Dick Lugar, the odds were strong that the Democrats would win. Immediately after the primary, Clark wanted to do something to unite the party. I happened to be the president of the Marion County Republican Veterans, which at the time was a very viable organization.

Alex suggested that we throw a picnic for the entire Republican organization. We did so at the Marion County Fairgrounds. We must have had a 100-percent attendance of precinct Committeeman and their Vices, as well as the Ward Chairs and Vice Chairmen. It seemed that the entire organization turned out to eat chicken and drink beer.

Alex gave a great speech on why we all must get behind Lugar. Dick and Keith were very gracious in welcoming all Republicans back in the fold. When we left that night, the party was united, and the beer was gone.

The Democrats, on the other hand, were still fighting with each other and did so all summer and fall.

Lugar won the fall election by about 9,000 votes.

The Innovative Security Operation

A large part of the credit for the 9,000-vote victory for Dick Lugar could be attributed to a well thought-out and innovative ballot security operation.

We knew we were getting rolled in some of the "fast Wards." We took the voter registration list and sent a letter, with first-class return postage guaranteed, to thousands of voters in the strong Democrat areas. Thousands of these letters were returned, marked Not at This Address, Deceased, No Such Address, Empty Lot, etc. As an example, there were multiple voters registered at the address of the White Castle burger joint at 16th and Illinois Streets.

After the envelopes were returned, we separated them by precinct and had the precinct committeeman try to check on those that said Empty Lot or No Such Address, or check whether the address was really a business.

On Election Day, we had recruited several hundred brave souls (lawyers and businessmen) to be at the polls at 6 a.m. with a stack of returned envelopes to challenge those that had shown up on our mailings. The challenge affidavits had been pre-prepared and stapled to the envelopes. I don't have to tell you this caused some problems. People don't like getting challenged by some dude they never saw before. There were some altercations.

The Republicans had the sheriff's office, and the Democrat mayor had the city police. At one point, where we had a lot of trouble, the city police car was parked at one end of the block, and the county sheriff's car was parked at the other end. It looked like we were going to have another "Shootout at the OK Corral." Certainly, the Lugar campaign was the beneficiary. We used this ballot security system for several elections after that.

Several years later, a federal law suit was filed, and the federal judge ruled that a returned envelope was not enough evidence to challenge a vote. I was one of the defendants.

A New Mayor and Racial Challenges

Dick's first term was in a period of racial unrest all across our country. Just a few months after Lugar took office, Bobby Kennedy was speaking at 17th and Broadway in Indianapolis. There he announced to a mostly African-American crowd that Dr. Martin Luther King, Jr. had been killed in Memphis. Feelings were running high.

With serious outbreaks of violence in Newark, New Jersey, Detroit, and other cities, Indianapolis was sitting on a powder keg. Lugar showed his mettle. He met the problem head-on with meetings and commitments. One of Lugar's innovations was his Lighted Schoolhouse program. Jim Morris played an important role in putting this program together. They organized dances, athletic events, and so on with supervised activities practically 24 hours per day. Dick somehow financed the programs with Indy Parks and Recreation Department money and donations. That summer had a few rumbles, even reports of shots being fired, but somehow Dick Lugar and his administration kept Indianapolis from turning into another Detroit.

Unigov and Doc's Phone Number

The 1971 election was coming up, and we all knew that lightning rarely strikes twice. The Democrat side was no longer fighting. That's when the best thing since buttered popcorn was conceived: namely, Unigov (county-wide government). Charley Whistler, Beurt SerVaas, Charlie Castor,

Keith, and others put it together along with Mayor Lugar. What a great idea. (Remember, 32 years of Republicans.)

Senator Dub Hill was the sponsor in the Republican-controlled senate, and it was passed in the senate and sent to the House where Otis "Doc" Bowen was the speaker. When the bill looked like it was being held by Doc, Lugar had a press conference giving out Doc's private phone number. This did not please Doc Bowen because he had all the senate-passed bills on his desk and was hearing them in the order they came over. Lugar took the blame publicly and didn't blame it on his staff. The bill passed with big numbers, and Governor Whitcomb signed it. Santa Claus came early to the Republicans that year.

The White Picket Fence Campaign

In 1971, Lugar beat John Neff approximately 150,000 to 100,000. Compare that with Lugar's 1967 election margin of approximately 9,000 votes (72,000 to 63,000). The 1972 mayor's race was a walkover from the start. John Neff, the Democrat candidate, and his consultants decided their campaign should be identified by the White Picket Fence. I really think this was to remind people that John Neff wanted to promote safe and secure neighborhoods. Whatever, his idea to use White Picket Fences backfired.

Our whole country had just gone through some racial strife. The African-American community saw the White Picket Fence as a message from John Neff that his administration wanted to cater to neighborhoods that were opposed to integration. I know that's a stretch, but perception in politics is everything. Of course, we did what we could to promote that perception.

In addition to all the suburban Republicans, who could now vote in a mayor's race (thanks to Unigov), Lugar did very well in the old inner city and in the African-American neighborhoods.

I saw Dr. Frank Lloyd, who would later become President of Methodist Hospital, work all day in the inner-city Wards promoting Lugar. Even the Black Panthers were promoting Lugar in the 6th Ward. Lugar won by an amazing margin.

Deal or No Deal?

Was there a deal made between Keith and some Democrats in 1967? I do not know. If there were, it sure was a great thing for Republicans. Think about it. A vibrant downtown, Circle Centre Mall, the Hoosier (RCA) Dome, the Colts, and other improvements might not have happened. Think about the Republicans having a mayor for 32 years.

I must admit that I did find it a little strange that Keith slated, nominated, and elected Jim Beatty's law partner to the state senate after Lugar's first election—especially because most of us in Republican politics had never hear of him.

Bulen Goes National

Keith loved three things: politics, standard-bred racing (you know, the one where horses pull the carts), and insulting people. As far as politics was concerned, when Keith was elected as Republican National Committeeman, he began to lose interest in local politics. He had a condo at the Watergate in Washington, DC and ran with the big dogs. His heart and soul was the national level, not Marion County.

With a Republican President (Nixon) and two Democrat Senators Birch Bayh and Vance Hartke, the Indiana Republican National Committeeman was the big kahuna in Indiana. The federal patronage flowed through Keith although Tabbert had some close friends in the Nixon administration and certainly had some influence.

Keith alienated Haldeman and John Ehrlichman, Nixon's two close advisors. Keith once proclaimed if Nixon had just one Precinct Committeeman from Marion County as an advisor instead of those two, Watergate would have never happened. Break into the Democrat Headquarters. How insane. What did they expect? To find their TV buys?

Spiro Agnew's Nabobs and Bribes

The 1968 Republican National Convention was held in Miami. I was having breakfast with Keith, and one of the National operatives came by and whispered in Keith's ear, "Spiro Agnew as Vice President". Keith could not believe it. I don't think Keith or I had ever heard of him.

After the 1968 elections, I was at a Republican gathering in Des Moines, Iowa. Agnew was the speaker. It was that speech where Agnew accused the national press as being "nattering nabobs of negativism." I thought to myself, that fellow has to be squeaky clean to take on the press like that. It wasn't too long that the press revealed Agnew had taken bribes while serving as governor of Maryland.

Bulen and Women

Despite being a brilliant political strategist and a tireless worker, Keith had his faults. Some how he and women just didn't always hit it off. Keith was married four times.

Shortly after Ed Whitcomb's election, an election that Keith helped put together, it was well known that Mrs. Whitcomb had already placed Keith on the "do not invite" list. I do know that when we had future President Ronald Reagan and Nancy Reagan at our house, Nancy balked at riding in the same car with Keith the night before plans were put together. (Keith did a great job for Reagan in the fall election. Keith was in charge of eight or 10 states in the northeast part of the country, which he carried.)

It probably wasn't a good idea on Keith's part to alienate the governor or the President's wife.

Will Rogers and Keith Bulen

Will Rogers was credited with saying, "I never met a man I didn't like." It was election night in 1980. Reagan had been declared the winner, and national TV was flashing the celebrations in various states. They showed one celebration (I think it was California), and there was a giant banner that read "WILL ROGERS NEVER MET KEITH BULEN." Keith had a national reputation of being hard to get along with after the Reagan campaign.

Friends

Despite arguing vehemently with Keith in the Legislature when we both served, despite me staying with Dale Brown and opposing Keith for County Chairman, despite bucking the slate and managing Alex Clark's campaign against Keith's candidate Dick Lugar, Keith and I remained friends.

In 1972, Doc Bowen, who disliked Keith, called me and wanted me to become part of his campaign for governor. I told Doc, "Even though I know you are going to win, Keith wants me to be for Bill Sharp, and that is what I'm going to do." Doc did win.

Keith was very prominent in my being appointed to the American Battle Monuments Commission by President Reagan. I served from 1982-1989.

Keith and The Star

Most of the time, Keith was in trouble with The Indianapolis Star. One evening at the Antelope Club, Keith had several cocktails and so had Bob Mooney, the political writer for The Star. Keith proclaimed that he, Keith Bulen, was running Marion County, and not Eugene Pulliam, the publisher of The Star. That was probably a bad move. In the 1961 session of the Legislature, The Star, with Bob Early (no relation), leading the way as editor, wanted the city to build a convention center. The bill did not pass, and Bob Early and The Star blamed Bulen. I remember after I was elected in 1962, we (the elected legislators) had a meeting with Bob Early, Gene Pulliam, and Bill Brooks. Bob Early was on Bulen like ugly on a monkey. He read him the Riot Act. It scared me. We passed a convention center bill in the 1963 session of the Legislature. There were lots of other occasions where Keith was on the front page of The Star.

Bulen, Hudnut, and a Wedding

The liquor license fiasco and campaign funds being misused were two of the longest-running stories. During one of the periods Keith was taking heat from The Star, Keith asked his honor, Mayor Hudnut, to perform the marriage ceremony for one of his daughters. Hudnut refused. If it had not been for Keith, there would have never been a Mayor Hudnut. It really hurt Keith's feelings.

Bill Hudnut had probably forgotten the George Washington Plunkitt advice, "It is important to be loyal to your friends—even up to the penitentiary door." I think Bill Hudnut regretted that decision later on.

Mayor Bill had the intestinal fortitude to promote the Circle Centre Mall and to build a football stadium before we had a football team. Both were gutsy moves. Yet he wouldn't marry Keith's daughter because the newspaper was banging on Keith.

Bulen and the Horses

Keith loved standard-bred horse racing. After a couple of tries, Keith bought a cheap yearling at the Lexington sales. The odds against this happening were enormous, but Keith's cheap horse became the world champion. He named it Abercrombie.

Keith, in his own humble, quiet way, let the world know (including the silk-stocking owner of the country's breeding farms) that he was the smartest and best authority on standard-bred horses in the world. To say that Keith wasn't very popular in the horse society is an understatement.

Keith had done it, and now he—and he alone—could pick horses at the big Lexington sales. Keith put together a partnership made up of himself, Gordon Tabor (who also owned horses), Kent Howard, Mike Maio, and me.

The big sale day came, and Keith picked two yearling fillies, out of good mares, and sired (of course) by the great Abercrombie. It was exciting to watch our two future world champions being broken and trained at the Indiana State

Fairgrounds. We were going to do so well. I just knew I could probably quit my job soon.

Because both horses were going to set the world on fire, we decided to ship them to Pinehurst in North Carolina. They had a great, although expensive, training facility. Our two champions could train all winter without worrying about snow at the Indiana State Fairgrounds. Bulen had a condo at Pinehurst where we stayed on our trips to watch our champions.

The Pinehurst Country Club clubhouse was strictly "deep south." It was very upscale, so you had to dress appropriately. Our group was eating dinner one night, and after a few cocktails, Bulen and Kent Howard got into an argument over whom Bulen was backing for Lt. Governor in the upcoming election. Bulen had committed to John Mutz, and Howard was a big Kermit Burrous supporter. The argument got loud and nasty, and we were asked to leave the country club.

Our horses were trained, and in early spring, they were shipped back to the fairgrounds. They looked sharp. They had been trained hard, and it was time to race them. Get the trophies and the purses ready because here we come!

There was one problem: Our two super horses couldn't beat Woody Burton. They were super slow. They had a hard time qualifying for any race, much less winning one. So much for our partnership. If you ever see an Amish horse and buggy going rather slow, it might be one of our fillies. It was expensive but fun to watch Bulen in action. He blamed everything on the trainer.

Early and the Horses

Later on, I bought an Indiana-bred, yearling filly and created my own partnership. It included Gordon Tabor (who picked out the filly), Mike Maio, John White (an attorney), Frank Otte (an attorney), Dr. Jim and Scotty Bennett, Henry and Nancy Blackwell, and me. Our horse was named Ravens Arrow. Among other races, she won the Indiana Sires Stakes for 2-year-olds in 1981, setting a new record that lasted for several years. She raced as a three-year-old, winning several times, and the Bennetts bought her to be a brood mare. She turned out several good race horses for them, and she is still alive and kicking on the Bennett farm. Ed Lewis, Evan Bayh's guru, also was in the standard-bred business. He and my wife owned a couple of horses together. The horses were nothing to brag about, but Ed was fun to be with.

Later, I bought a nice, yearling filly sired by Windshield Wiper, as a Christmas present for my wife. She was big and ugly (the filly, not my wife) and was not a great racer. She was bred to Bo Bo Arrow, who had the same sire as Ravens Arrow. The first foal she named Paine in the Bo Bo, and it turned out to be a really good horse. She raced him mostly in Chicago. He won 11 races and got a check (finished in the top five) 57 times out of 62 races. He was retired to a farm near Noblesville. We had to have him castrated before anyone would take him. (They get a little mean if not gelded.) He is still not speaking to us.

Chapter 6
Marion County Politics

The Indianapolis Star was on a rampage! It seems that people were getting their license plates without paying their property taxes (which then included your personal property). The Indianapolis Star wrote about this grave injustice for a couple of weeks.

Noble Pearcy was our Prosecutor. Not wanting to get cross-ways with The Star, Prosecutor Pearcy announced that anyone who had, or was getting, a license plate had better have a "stamped receipt" from the County Treasurer's office, or they would be charged with a crime. This caused quite an uproar.

Actual lines of people stood on Delaware Street, almost to Ohio Street. There were arguments and basically a bunch of pissed-off people. All of them were trying to get their stamp at the Treasurer's office.

You Want Your Stamp Now?

The Democrats held the Treasurer's office. John Dobkins was treasurer. He had hired lots of extra help, including one of my friends, Kevin White, who was a city fireman, working there on his off days. The Marion County Treasurer's Office was stayed open late. Kevin had been there all day.

An irate taxpayer came in to get his stamp. He told Kevin what he thought of bureaucrats, explained how many hours he stood in line, and said, "I want my stamp, and I want it now, and I don't want any BS from you!" Kevin replied, "You want your stamp now?" Then Kevin grabbed him, wrestled him to the floor, stamped his head, his shirt, and was trying to stamp him again when they pulled Kevin off.

The Antelope Club and the Shoe Stamp

Another character who worked in the City-County Building hung around the Antelope Club. Somehow, he had procured one of the rubber stamps that were being used in the Treasurer's office. He had the rubber stamp sewn into his gym shoe. For 10 bucks, he stepped on your tax receipt, which gave a visible print of the paid stamp. A real entrepreneur, he had several customers at the Antelope Club. I did notice when he stepped on a receipt, he kept his head and eyes looking straight ahead. He wanted it to look like if he stepped on somebody's receipt, it was an accident.

I don't know how he would have explained his gym shoe.

Arrest That Kangaroo!

In 1974, the Democrats controlled the Clerk's office and the Election Board. A story had been in The Star about our candidate for sheriff accepting a campaign contribution from a well-known Democrat (Diamond Don Gilman).

The contribution was in cash and came out of the freezer of a refrigerator. The press liked to talk about it being "cold cash."

Because the Democrats controlled the election board, they decided they would subpoena Republicans, and in general, make the election board meetings a circus for the press. They were having fun with Jud Haggerty, a real bright and funny guy, as chairman. The election board meetings were held often, and they were turning it into a circus, with the Republicans being the bad guys. I decided it was a kangaroo court and had said so. After a few meetings, I rented a kangaroo costume, complete with a kangaroo head, and hired a buddy of mine (for $25) to hop through their next meeting. He did and was hilarious. Haggerty was yelling, "Arrest that, that...animal!" The press was having a field day as chaos prevailed. TV cameras recorded the event. I told two of the reporters, Art Harris and Gerry Lafollette, what I was going to do. There was a little problem when their editor and boss told them to find out who was responsible for this. They couldn't find him. It worked out better than I dreamed. That was their last meeting of the kangaroo court.

Chapter 7
Bill Jenner (My Hero)

In 1976, the Republican National Convention was held at Kansas City. Ronald Reagan won the Indiana primary, beating the sitting President, Gerald Ford. The question was, who was the convention going to choose? The sitting President, or Ronald Reagan? The vote was close. Of course, President Ford had control over the National Committee Chairman, and thus, the convention management.

The Former Senator,
the Vice President, and a Lot of Yelling

After a lot of negotiations, it was decided rather than have a straight vote of Reagan versus Ford, the delegates would vote on some innocuous resolution. If you were for Reagan, vote yes. If for Ford, vote no. After the resolution was offered, the national chairman called a recess. The Ford forces were ready. They had a dossier on all the delegates, and they sent their troops into each state delegation. Elliot Richardson and Secretary of Agriculture Earl Butz, Bill Ruckelshaus, and others worked the Indiana delegation.

I was sitting on the floor with Seth Denbo, Paul Green, John Snyder, and Senator Bill Jenner. All of us were for Reagan. Seth had given one of the 8th District delegate seats to a person we had never heard of. We had no idea whether he was a Reagan vote or a Ford vote, although Seth assured us he was okay. Seth's delegate was sitting about three rows in front of us, and we saw Nelson Rockefeller sitting with him, his arm around his shoulder, and they were both laughing and having a good old time. Now Rockefeller, besides being one of the wealthiest people in the country, was our Vice President.

When Jenner saw this, he jumped up and started yelling obscenities at Nelson Rockefeller. Among other things Jenner yelled, "We ran your ass out of Indiana in 1964!" (This was when Rockefeller wanted to run for President against Goldwater.) Jenner finished by saying, "You weren't welcome then, and you're not welcome now."

It was obvious to me that Nelson Rockefeller had never been called these names to his face. In fact, some of Jenner's message probably contained words he had never heard before. I'm sure that Rockefeller had no idea that it was a former United States Senator yelling at him. In any event, Rockefeller decided he could probably find more fertile ground than in Indiana. Jenner, upon expressing his opinion, sat back down and started talking like nothing happened.

Those Beautiful Damned Bricks

My engineering company, Mid States Engineering, got the contract from the city for the beautification of the Monument Circle, the centerpiece of downtown Indianapolis.

That is when the bricks were put in place. I had gone into the Antelope Club for lunch and was sitting down at the bar when I heard this loud voice saying, "Early, is that you?" Jenner was at a table in the dining room with Seth and John Snyder. At this time, Jenner was getting up in age and had some sight problems. I sat down with them, and Jenner said to me, "Early, you know what's going on in Indianapolis, and I want to know something. What crooked son of a bitch is responsible for tearing up the Circle and putting those bricks in? Those concrete sidewalks and streets would have lasted 100 years, and now they're tearing it out! I can't even walk from my office to the Columbia Club without stepping in a hole or stumbling over those damn bricks." At that point, John Snyder poked Jenner with his elbow and said, "It's Rex's company that is doing that!" Jenner thought for a minute and said, "Boy, that thing's going to be beautiful when it's finished."

George Washington Plunkitt once said, "Patronage should be honored as the supreme form of patriotism." Bill Jenner, I'm sure, agreed.

Holding Out for Holder

Bill was nominated and elected as a United States Senator while he was still in the Army. Bill was Mr. Conservative; one of his best pals in the Senate was Senator Joe McCarthy. Bill told me the story of how Cale Holder became a judge. Both Bill and Cale were organization Republicans, and both served as the Republican State Chairman. Both had opposed Eisenhower at the national convention.

Because Jenner had so openly opposed Eisenhower, someone from the national media asked Jenner, "How can you now support Eisenhower after opposing him so strongly at the convention?"

Jenner replied, "Comparing Eisenhower to Adlai Stevenson is like comparing chicken salad to chicken shit!"

After Eisenhower was elected, Bill set out to get his pal, Cale Holder, the federal judgeship in Indiana's Southern District.

President Eisenhower's great friend and military cohort was General George Marshall. There were reasons that Senator Jenner disliked Marshall. General Marshall, of course, was put in charge of the Marshall Plan, whose mission was to rebuild bombed-out Europe.

At some point, Jenner, on the floor of the Senate, described General Marshall as a "living lie." This, of course, did not go over big with President Eisenhower.

At one point, Sherman Adams, one of President Eisenhower's trusted aides, called on Jenner in his office. He told Jenner that the only way that Cale Holder would ever become a judge is when Senator Jenner made a public apology to General George Marshall. Jenner asked whether Adams had ever heard or read Jenner's speech about Marshall. When Adams said no, Jenner asked his secretary to get Adams a copy. Upon reading the speech, Adams said, "My God, Senator! This is even worse than I imagined!"

And Jenner said, "And I meant every word of it, and I will never apologize!" In the meantime, the Attorney General hired one of the Indianapolis law firms, now Barnes and Thornburg, to dig up what they could on Holder.

The Indianapolis Star also ran some articles that were detrimental to Holder.

The standoff went on. Holder wasn't appointed, but no

other judges had been confirmed by the Senate. Finally, Senator Jenner was called by the President to The White House. During their conversation, Jenner told the President that his very good friend, Senator James Eastland, a Southern Democrat who was chairman of the Senate Judiciary Committee, had assured Jenner that until Cale Holder was appointed judge in Indiana, there would be no other hearings for any judgeship in the country.

Jenner won, and Cale Holder was appointed federal judge by President Eisenhower. Eisenhower also appointed Don Tabbert, a Holder and Jenner friend, as the U.S. District Attorney for the Indiana Southern District.

Did He Really Say That?

Bill Jenner was the greatest stump speaker who ever graced Indiana politics. When he jerked off his coat, took off his tie, and rolled up his sleeves, you were about to hear how the liberals and the dirty, rotten Communists were going to destroy this great country. (He was my hero!)

His vocabulary was a little salty at times. When he talked about "Vanderburgh Vance," (Senator Hartke, who filled Jenner's seat when he stepped down by beating Jenner's pal, Harold Handley), it was like venom coming out of his mouth. In one speech, he said that Hartke was "a pimple on the prick of progress." He accused another person as being "thinner than cow piss on a flat rock."

Can you imagine Senator Lugar saying that? Bill Jenner was the only person who could get by with that, and the Republicans loved him.

I heard a Doc Bowen speech one night where Doc had obviously lost a couple of pages of his written speech. It made no sense, but Doc went right ahead without noticing. It was okay, though. Most of the audience didn't notice it, either. Doc Bowen often joked that the only way to stay awake during a Doc Bowen speech is to give it. No one ever said that about Bill Jenner's speeches.

Needless to say, Senator Jenner and Doc had different speaking styles.

The Speaker Is Smart

After Jenner left the Senate, he remained a sought-after speaker for political audiences.

Jenner was the speaker at a Mid-West College Republican conference, which was held in the Claypool Hotel. The Rockefeller forces and the Goldwater forces were at each other's throats, each vying for leadership positions. The Rockefeller delegates knew that Jenner was for Goldwater. They also knew that Jenner was a very close friend of Senator Joe McCarthy. The Rockefeller forces heard that Jenner was going to praise McCarthy in his speech. They were all set to, "Boo" when Senator McCarthy's name was mentioned.

Jenner said, "There was a man who walked on this Earth and led many people to see problems in our world. This man was betrayed by his friends. And this man was Jesus Christ."

Even the Rockefeller supporters had to cheer at that line after being prepared to boo the name they expected—Joe McCarthy.

Chapter 8
The Republican Veterans

After World War II, Indiana politics were dominated by the veterans who came home after the war. As a Republican, you had to have the backing of the state American Legion organization if you were running for a state office. George Craig's nomination and election as governor in 1950 was helped tremendously by his friends who were involved with American Legion politics. In Marion County, Alex Clark, Cale Holder, Ed Steers, and others put together an organization called the Republican Veterans. When I became involved as a member in 1958, the Republican Veterans were still a dominant force. Because many of them were lawyers, they had a lot of influence on who our judicial candidates were.

At the same time, by 1958, the political muscle of the American Legion was diminishing. Besides having a board meeting and some money, we had two activities. One was an October party for the entire Republican organization. We all sold tickets to our mummy-dummies and used the money from the ticket sales to buy door prizes to be given out at the summer party. With 900-plus precinct committeemen and another 900-plus vice-committeemen, as well as ward and ward vice-chairmen, political hanger-ons, and wannabes, we had big crowds. We fed them chicken and beer and gave out door prizes. The organization people were mailed "free tickets."

Alex Clark would usually handle the door prizes. He pulled a name out of the hat and read off a name of some precinct committeeman who Alex recognized, usually an old timer, and who appreciated the door prize. The door prizes were usually fruit baskets (made at the City Market) or hams. Most of the door prize winners were from the inner city.

The other activity was a summer party (males only) out at German Park. Several hundred attended, and if some candidate wanted to speak, it better be a short speech.

The Poker Game

Also starting about 6 in the evening, we had a poker game. It started out fairly cheap, at $1 and $2. At 8 o'clock, it would go to $2 and $5. At 10 o'clock, it would be $5 and $10 dollars—and soon after that, it was bet what you wanted to. (No limit.) It was about midnight, and the game was on. Keith Bulen, who was a bad player even when he was sober, had had a few drinks. In fact, he had his own bottle. Kit Carson, Charley Castor, Jim Bradford, P.K. Ward, a Mr. Stevenson (whose wife was Prosecutor Noble Pearcy's secretary), and me were some of the participants that I remember. The poker players were the only ones left, and we were in an open shelter house out in the middle of a woods a long way from the highway.

Three Young Dudes and One Gun

One of us looked up and saw three young, tough-looking dudes, all with their hands in their pockets. There was a lot of money on the table, and we were about to get robbed. I was sitting next to Mr. Stevenson, who had eased a pistol out of his pocket and was holding it in his lap. It occurred to me and my razor-sharp mind that I was going to be in the middle of a gun fight, and I didn't have my gun. Mr. Stevenson was probably in his late sixties or seventies and had probably had a nice long life. I had just passed 30. I must admit I was as nervous as a pig at a packing plant.

About that time, Bulen, in his somewhat inebriated state, looked at them and asked, "What in the hell are you doing here?" and then called one by name. As it turned out, Bulen had represented one or two of them on some strong-arm charge not long before that. One replied, "Hello, Mr. Bulen." They had two choices: Get out of there, or shoot us all. They chose to move on. God bless L. Keith Bulen.

He Needs a Doctor

Another memorable event was when Bob Gates (a Republican District Chairman) passed out. Gates' father, Ralph Gates, had been Governor of Indiana. It was a very hot day, and Gates had on a suit and tie. I think he had just gotten too hot. In any event, he was lying on the ground, and a crowd had gathered.

Alex Clark was kneeling down, trying to loosen his tie and collar. Alex yelled out, "Is there a doctor around?" Someone said, "Here is Doc Hemphill." Now Doc Hemphill was a chiropractor who had been one of Dale Brown's best friends and was a Marion County Commissioner. Alex

73

looked up at Doc Hemphill and said, "The man don't need nothing stolen; he needs a doctor!" Obviously, Alex was not a great admirer of Doc Hemphill's when he was a County Commissioner.

When I ran for governor, Jim Clark got a phone call from Ed Steers' law firm. It seems that Ed had been treasurer of the veterans, and still had a few thousand dollars in the bank. We had a meeting of all three of us and voted to give the money to my campaign. The vote was unanimous. That closed out the veterans, who hadn't met for years.

Chapter 9
Stan Strader, Seth Denbo, and Jack Hesseldenz

Stan Strader

Stan Strader is my pal. He is an African-American, a former Marine, and a good guy. His father was "Fat Cat," a Republican Precinct Committeeman around Barrington Heights, also called Love Town, on the near south side of Indianapolis.

The Young Lions

During the '60s, Stan helped start and lead an organization called the Watoto Simbas (the Young Lions). Stan was an imposing figure at six-foot five-inches with a .50 caliber machine gun bullet he picked up in the Marine Corps that hung around his neck with some lion's teeth. He also wore a lion skin around his shoulders.

Stan's Watotos, who supported Lugar in his first election, numbered about 50 at that time. But Stan and the Watotos had some requests of the mayor's office. As a matter of fact, they pressured for and finally got a health clinic in Barrington. Also, they were successful in securing a drug clinic in the same area. With the mayor's assistance, they got some help from Lilly Endowment, which included some help with the parks in their area. Basically, the Watotos was an African-American organization that was interested in the Barrington Heights area.

I first met Stan at a political gathering when I was the Center Township Chairman. I talked to him about running for office. Being a former Marine, I liked Stan from the first time I ever met him. Paul Cantwell, a Democrat leader, occupied the City-Council seat in that district for several years. It was probably a 70/30 Democratic district with no hope of ever electing a Republican. Paul decided not to run, and another Democrat lady was picked to take over that seat.

Against the Odds

I asked Stan to run. He agreed, and this started a campaign which was absolutely the most fun that I've ever been associated with (as far as campaigns go). First of all, the district was split by Raymond Street. On the south side of Raymond Street, it was predominately white and included the Garfield Park area. It was the 30th Ward. The north side, however was predominately African-American: the 17th Ward.

Several public housing projects were in the area, including the two at Emerson and Raymond. The Democrat candidate, as I said, was a Caucasian lady who worked for the Catholic Youth Organization (CYO). I don't remember her last name, but Bernadette was her first name. She was really a nice lady.

Stanley assembled his troops, and what an assembly it was! There was "Bump" (all four-foot five-inches tall of him), "Snake," "Fat Cat," "Corky," and "Baby Boy." And at that time, I had an Election Day driver and sort of a bodyguard named "Kid Dynamite" who also worked with me on that campaign. Most of them lived near or in the projects.

We decided early on that Stan's push would be the Projects and the African-American community where he grew up. He would leave the south side of his district, south of Raymond Street alone. We left that to the Republican organization to deliver. On the south side, there would be no yard signs with Stanley's picture.

Republican Headquarters and the mayor's office said we were just wasting our time; that we were out of our mind; that there was no way that we could win. Jim Clark, Murray's father, and I did our best to help finance the campaign.

Lo and behold, and against all odds, Stanley won! Part of it might have been because no one could find "Ground Hog." Ground Hog was also an African-American and the Democrat Ward Chairman. Something happened, and he disappeared on Election Day. In fact, he was harder to find that day than Jimmy Hoffa.

Six Legs

At one point on that Election Day, I picked up Mike DeFabis, Deputy Mayor and Republican activist. We visited the Pride Community Center. (I just want any of you to try to find that: the Pride Community Center.)

When Mike and I went in, we could see six legs inside the voting machine curtain. Mike was beside himself, saying, "Let's call the election board! Let's call the sheriff!

Let's call the police! They're cheating us!" I told Mike to forget it (in case they were our six legs). I did not want to know whether they were theirs or ours. Stan Strader won the election.

Four More Years

Guess what! Four years later, Stan ran again. The Democrats certainly knew our strategy, and they were not going to be blindsided this time. Nobody gave us a chance. Joe Slash, Republican Deputy Mayor under Lugar, said we had no chance and not to waste any money on that campaign.

Guess what! Stanley, Fat Cat, Baby Boy, Corky, Snake, Bump, ad infinitum . . . the guys did it again. Stanley was a knowledgeable and a good councilman. He left the council to take a federal job. He's a great guy and a good friend.

Quality of Life

Before Stan left the council, he became very involved in trying to get something done about the deplorable state of some of our public housing projects. With his urging, the council created a citizen's committee to look into the problem. Stan insisted that I be on the commission and act as co-chairman.

Upon examination of the Projects, it was really worse than any of us had been told. Most of the apartments were uninhabitable. Martha Lamkin was the head of the Indiana HUD office. Because of the lack of management, she had cut off all HUD funds for maintenance.

Mayor Hudnut appointed me to the Board of the Public Housing authority. I pressed our manager to resign; when that happened, the whole board quit. Hudnut issued me a new appointment document that said I was The Board. I still have it.

In any event, we hired new management, enlarged our committee with several community leaders (Tom Binford was one), and got HUD to turn loose the maintenance funds.

In the next year, practically all of the units were remodeled. The mayor helped by shifting city policemen to help with security and ordered the Board of Public Works to get involved with cleaning up the grounds. A new board was appointed, and the corporate community helped in various ways to stabilizing the Projects.

Stan Strader, as a City-County Councilman, made a big difference in the quality of life for a lot of poor people. How many office holders can say that?

Seth Denbo

Seth was one of the last of the real Republican good old boys whose personal philosophy mirrored such heroes as George Washington Plunkitt and Dick Daley. As a matter of fact, it was Plunkitt who said, "It is important to be loyal to your friends, even up to the penitentiary door."

Seth was from English, Indiana, right down the road from Marengo. And he reigned as the Republican 8th District Chairman. In order to get to Seth's house, you went up a steep hill on the road. At the top of the hill, a billboard offered the message, "Prepare to meet thy God!" Seth lived in the next house.

Steamed Ballots and Egg Whites

Ken Bode was the political analyst for the NBC network. He had come to Indiana to report on the 8th District

Congressional race in 1984. The race was between Rick McIntyre and Frank McCloskey. The recount committees could never agree on who won the race. Tip O'Neill had seated McCloskey (a Democrat) proclaiming he had won by four votes.

Bode said he and his TV crew were close to English, Indiana, so he decided to talk to Seth. He told his crew, "This will last only five minutes, and then we will be out of there!" Bode spent three hours with Seth. Bode was fascinated. Seth started out by telling Bode how easy it was to negate an absentee ballot.(Now he didn't say he did it; he just said it was easy.) You went to the clerk's office and steamed opened the envelope with the ballot in it. If it was a vote against you, you marked up the ballot so it would be thrown out—like voting for two candidates for the same office. Then you resealed the envelope, using egg white. Seth said that egg white worked best because you couldn't spot it. During their conversation, Seth was damning the Democrats from his district. Seth said you could not trust them. As an example, Seth said they had been paying $3 per vote for years, and the Democrats had raised it to $4 without telling Seth.

Seth was upset about such a breach of ethics.

And the Name Is . . .

Seth called me one day for a favor. This was during the Bowen administration. He lamented the fact that his best buddy was having a hard time getting a state permit to haul coal.

Seth wanted me to call one of the commissioners of the Indiana State Commerce Commission. He found out that one of the commissioners was from Indianapolis, and I knew him.

I wavered, saying, "Seth, I don't know him all that well."

Seth wouldn't give up. He said he knew this buddy in kindergarten and went all through school with him. He said they were the best man in the each other's weddings. Seth said they joined the military together. Furthermore, if his pal didn't get his permit, Seth would be forced to quit because his friend was the largest contributor to the Republican party in the whole 8th District.

I couldn't stand to hear a grown man cry. I said, "Okay, Seth, what's his name?" There was deathly silence, and I could hear paper being shuffled. Finally Seth said, "I've lost my notes, and I'll have to call you back."

I always wondered since why Seth couldn't remember his best friend's name. Just maybe, Seth was doing a little lobbying for a fee.

Seth was a notorious bad driver. One night going home from Indianapolis to English, he reportedly went off the road, hit a light pole, and blacked out the Columbus-Seymour football game.

When Seth passed, Governor Bob Orr went to the funeral. He was quoted as saying he "hadn't come to mourn; he came to make sure."

May Seth rest in peace. He was one of a kind.

What Day?

Seth's successor in Crawford County was Kirsten Corbett. Now Kirsten had a small speech impediment. (He couldn't pronounce the letter L.) We had a statewide seminar of Republican leaders. Bud Gohmann and I spoke about ballot security.

Being from Seth's Crawford County, Kirsten was an active participant in that discussion.

He reported some of the irregularities he had observed in the last "erection." He had all kinds of stories about past "erections." So as not to embarrass Kirstin, Bud and I joined in about what you should do on "erection" day.

Judge Jack Hesseldenz
(General Dillon once accused Hessie of dressing like a "color-blind pimp.")

Along with Bud Gohmann and Jim Clark, Jack Hesseldenz was the kind of friend you wanted if you were out in a fox hole and people were shooting at you. Hessie, as he was called, had a great sense of humor. He was the Center Township Small Claims Court judge for years and years. Because his office was in the City-County Building, he was very close to where the marriage licenses were obtained. They got the marriage license on the main floor, and the judge would marry them in the basement. He must have performed 1,000 marriages down in his office.

The Judge's Ceremonies
If I happened to walk in while the judge was marrying, he would ask, "Do you, John Doe, take this woman before God and Rex Early to be your wife?" The answer was always yes.

The Dad, The Dame, and the Dandy
I was in his office waiting for him to go play golf while

he was performing a marriage. The bride was about eight months pregnant. A monstrous man, probably six-and-a-half feet tall and well over 300 pounds, was sitting there with a mean look on his face. He was obviously the father of the bride. The husband, on the other hand, was a slight fellow with real-pointy shoes. (Hessie liked to point out that those guys with real-pointy shoes could kill cockroaches in the corner.) But anyway, even with the 300-pound father, and despite his glaring, the wedding went on. When the future husband was asked whether he would he take this woman for better or for worse, the husband jumped in the air, did a complete 360-degree pirouette and sang out, "And it can't get no worse!"

The Watch Ceremony

I witnessed a wedding where Hessie asked the groom whether he had a ring. The groom said, no, he had a watch. Hessie asked him whether this was a single-watch ceremony or a double-watch ceremony. And in Hessie's style, when he read the marriage vows, he said, "With this watch, I thee wed." As I said, Hessie had a little sense of humor.

Oh, THAT Tommy Newman

Hessie and I had a buddy, Tommy Newman, who had recently married. He told us that he was driving down Michigan Street and stopped at a stoplight. He said he felt like somebody was looking at him. He looked at the car next to him, and it was his new in-laws.

As it happened, he had a young lady in the car with him. He was caught. The in-laws were glaring at him, but his razor-sharp mind came up with a solution. He signaled them to roll down their window. When they did, he announced, "I'm the guy who looks like Tommy Newman." And then he drove off. (I just gave him the name Tommy Newman.)

Chapter 10
Playing Hardball

Vance Hartke, a Democrat, was Indiana's U.S. senator. Ed Lewis was one of his friends. Vance sat on the Senate Committee that governed the REMCs (rural electricity companies).

Ed Lewis, my pal and a Democrat powerhouse, had a relationship with Hoosier Energy, which is an REMC generating company. Ed and some partners were in the coal mining business, and they sold coal to Hoosier Energy.

Hoosier Energy wanted to expand and build another generating plant. At that time, Public Service Company of Indiana (PSI) was a competitor of Hoosier Energy and probably didn't want them to build it. The Republican party wanted to beat Vance Hartke.

A Local Bugging

These are the facts as I know them. I do not know for what reason Ed Lewis' office got bugged, but I'm sure it had something to do with the coal and the competing energy companies. Were the people who ordered the bugging after Hartke? Were they trying to stop a new plant by REMC? Were they after Ed?

Ed blamed Keith Bulen and Charley Castor for masterminding the bugging. I think Bulen was too smart for that. In any event, an executive of PSI as well as the managing partner of one of our city's largest law firms were accused of hiring a private investigator to bug Ed Lewis' office.

As I said, I don't have a clue what they were looking for. Obviously, nothing criminal turned up in the way of recorded conversations, as far as I know.

Ed found out about the bugging when he ordered all new office furniture. He had the old furniture stacked in the hall with instructions for the clean-up crew to take the old furniture if they wanted it or to just get rid of it. The next day, one of the clean-up people came to Ed's office with a device in her hand that looked like a microphone. She found it attached to the bottom of the seat in one of the big chairs in Ed's office. She wanted to know whether this belonged to Ed. When she took Ed out to show him where she had found it, someone had drawn a bug on the bottom of the seat, with the word BUG inscribed next to where the microphone was. (How's that for rubbing it in?)

Some way, somehow, the people who were responsible were identified or at least accused of the dastardly deed. I remember the day of one of our Hog Nut parties. Ed Lewis had just come in, and he was smiling from ear to ear. His civil suit against the people who bugged him had been settled. He wouldn't tell me the amount of the settlement. I heard through the grapevine that it was gigantic.

How dumb can you be? And nobody went to jail?

Chapter 11
Senator Richard Lugar

I met Dick Lugar in 1967. Dick appeared at the Republican Screening Committee. The Committee was appointed by Keith Bulen to interview and pick a candidate for mayor. Little did any of us know that the person who was picked, Dick Lugar, would someday not only be a national figure but also an international figure.

Smart and Tough

I had heard that Bulen guaranteed Dick a "walk in the park" as far as the primary was concerned. When Alex Clark filed against Dick, it turned out to be a full-scale war.

During that primary, I found out that Dick was not only a fighter, but he was smarter than Norman Einstein. (He was a cousin of Albert Einstein.) Dick's work in the Senate, in both the agricultural area and in foreign affairs, is respected by both sides of the aisle. When Ronald Reagan was President, Dick Lugar had a higher percentage of voting for the Reagan Revolution and Reagan's programs than any other senator.

In 1980, Dick Lugar came very close to being Ronald Reagan's running mate. Lugar has not only served his country as a United States Senator, but he also served as a U.S. Naval officer. I have found that Dick and his Chief of Staff, Marty Morris, have always been most helpful, anytime I or any of his constituents had a problem.

Using Connections in a Good Way

I am reminded of one instance in 1990. My great friend, Alex Clark, a former Indianapolis mayor and Dick's first primary opponent, had been on a cruise in South America. Alex fell, due to some rough ocean, and died the next day from his head injury. The boat put in at the closest port, which was in Chile.

His brother, Jim, and Jim's son Murray, were at the Daytona 500 with me. Jim went home, got his passport, and headed toward Chile. Jim found that because of rules and bureaucracy, it was almost impossible to get Alex's body back to the United States. One call to Lugar, a member of the Foreign Relations Committee, and was it done in a few hours.

Recently, Senator Lugar helped get my lovely granddaughter, Emily, get into Denison University, Dick's alma mater. (I hope she learns as much as Dick did!) Being a right-wing hully-gully, I have not always agreed with Dick on 100 percent of his stands on issues. (Probably, I agreed 98 percent, but not 100 percent.)

He Shows Up at the Showdown

However, as one of my Marine Corps buddies from Texas said, "It is how you show up at the showdown that counts." Dick Lugar is always there at the showdown, doing the right thing. In 1994, when Dick ran for re-election, he named Mitch Daniels and me as co-chairmen of his campaign. Also, in January of 1996, I flew out to Iowa to help when Dick was one of the candidates for President in the Iowa caucus.

Chapter 12
Bud Gohmann

Bud Gohmann is one of my very best pals. He was a Deputy Sheriff (scary isn't it?), Marion County Clerk for eight years, and County Assessor for 12 years. Bud was just out of the Army when I first met him. Bud's father and grandmother were very active in the Republican Party, and Bud followed in their shoes.

Dale Brown had asked Bud (who later became chairman of the Young Republicans) to help me.

I was running for the Indiana state Legislature, and he asked Bud to take me to the Ward meetings on the south side of the city. I was fairly new on the block, and Bud knew most of the Ward Chairmen. Bud introduced me to most of the players and asked for their support. He did a good job, and I got nominated. Everyone loved Bud. At the same time, Bud was also running for office.

Running in a primary in those days was unbelievable. It was an endless round of Ward meetings. The usual procedure was as follows: Anywhere from 10–50 voters attending these meetings: mostly precinct committeeman, vice committeemen, poll-watchers, and patronage workers.

In addition to the Ward people, there were the wannabe candidates for township offices, county offices, judicial offices, state offices, and usually between 70 and 80 candidates for the Legislature. If you were an incumbent liked by the Ward Chairman, you got to speak early. If not, you got your one or two minutes at 11 p.m. or later.

Tell Them What They Want to Hear

We candidates all traveled around together and got to know each other's speeches by heart. In 1962, Bud Gohmann was running for Center Township Assessor. Bud, or any Republican, had no chance of being elected in Center Township, but we had to have a candidate. Bud knew that but gave it his best shot. One night, our traveling road show appeared before the Fraternal Order of Clubs Association. This group had representatives from the American Legion, the VFW, Moose, Eagles, Elks, etc.

The Indianapolis Star had been running a series about all the property tax exemptions, suggesting that clubs should not be exempt from property taxes. Bud gave a rip-roaring speech before this group, guaranteeing them if nominated and elected, he would stand with them against all the evil forces trying to end their exemptions. At the end, he got a standing ovation.

The very next night, we appeared in a strong Republican Ward where high property tax was their number-one issue. Bud's speech blasted those immoral interests that took these exemptions, and thus made higher taxes for homeowners.

If nominated and elected, Bud guaranteed he would fight till he dropped to end the exemptions. He got a standing ovation.

The candidates who were listening, of course, had heard both speeches. After the meeting, we asked Bud about this obvious 180-degree change in speeches.

Bud gave us his contagious Irish grin and said, "Boys, you got to tell them what they want to hear!" Good advice.

Bud, of course, was not elected in 1962, because the Democrats controlled Center Township. About this time, Bud went on the Sheriff's Department as a deputy.

The Sheriff and the Missing Child

I was riding in Bud's sheriff car one day when he was off duty, and a radio call came through about a missing child. We were close to the location, so Bud went over there. Several deputies were on the scene. Bud, being a captain, was the ranking officer there. Bud identified himself to the distraught parents. You could see by the look in their eyes: "At last! A captain who must be experienced in situations like this!!" Their relief was evident. Bud, in his best law enforcement manner, asked the parents to tell him all of the facts: when the child was last seen, what she was wearing, who were her friends, etc.

You could just see Bud's investigative mind at work as he digested all of the information. His mind was at work, and there has never been even a TV policeman who looked more professional as he or she solved a crime. Finally, after Bud mulled all the facts through, he asked, "Did you look under the bed?" The parents looked at Bud like he was a few pickles short of a barrel. Not long after that the little girl was found. She had been asleep on a neighbor's porch furniture. In 1978, Bud was nominated and elected as County Clerk.

The Randomee Clerk

The clerk's office is where all the lawsuits are filed. The rule was that as they filed a case, attorneys got a random draw for which court and which judge it would go in. Upon being elected clerk, Bud declared himself as the "Randomee." Now Bud wasn't the Randomee on all the filings, but he was the Randomee for the lawyers he liked. The goofs and some of the big law firm lawyers—the silk-stocking guys—still drew their courts on a random basis. So Bud was a part-time Randomee.

Bud really had no choice but to be the Randomee. The Honorable Frank Huse, the Marion County Circuit Court Judge, told Bud if he EVER again put another case where a certain female attorney was involved, he (Judge Huse) would sentence Bud to 30 days in jail.

The whole purpose of the random drawing was to evenly distribute the case loads between the various courts. If the last attorney drew Superior Court 3, there is nothing that says the next attorney has to draw Superior Court 4 if he don't like that judge. Bud could probably tell him to just wait around before filing. I ain't saying Bud did that. I said he "could have." As you might imagine, this made Bud a very popular guy with about half the attorneys.

The Little Sisters of the Poor

Bud and I had a lot of things in common. We were both Catholics and loved the Little Sisters of the Poor. Usually just before Christmas, the Sisters called on Bud and me for a donation, and we always complied. We wanted to do more for the Sisters. We invited one of the nuns, who literally begged on the streets, to come over to the City-County

Building just before Christmas. Bud and I and the Sister set up shop just outside the door of the clerk's office. Bud and I corralled the attorneys as they passed and suggested that they might want to donate to the Little Sisters of the Poor.

You'd be surprised how many of them really did want to donate to the Little Sisters of the Poor. When asked by the Randomee to give generously, they gave generously. We also had a rule: No change given. If they had only a fifty or a hundred-dollar bill, that was their tough luck. God bless the Little Sisters of the Poor! We thank them for looking after Bud and me all these years.

One year, in October, one of the Sisters came by my office. The Sisters were having a raffle for a new car. She asked whether I would sell a couple-hundred dollars' worth of tickets. I said sure. Just before the pre-Christmas drawing, she called to pick up my money. I had put them in my desk and hadn't sold one. I bought all 200 tickets. And I won the car.

The Slating Fee

Every four years, when Bud had to run, I was his campaign manager. As did all candidates, Bud had to pay a slating fee to the Marion County Republican Party. The slating fee was about ten percent of the first year's salary. For many of Bud's elections, I sent out a fundraising letter to help Bud pay his slating fee.

The letter went like this: "Bud is sending this letter to his 60 best friends. Because his slating fee is $6,000, it would be nice if each of you, his 60 best friends (mostly lawyers), would donate $100 to the Bud Gohmann campaign." We sent the letter to more than 100 people, and we usually raised over $10,000. Bud opened the envelopes and thus got "first count," so I will take his word for the amount. One person sent $400 with a note that he would be surprised if Bud had 60 friends.

Dusty Cancels The Star

Bud had a brother, Dusty, who was a policeman. Bud's brother had the Massachusetts Avenue District on the night shift. While working that shift, he became infatuated with a young lady who frequented the bars on Massachusetts Avenue. The young lady was physically challenged. She could not hear or talk. They communicated by passing notes to each other. It seems that one night, the two of them had a lover's spat.

It was pouring down rain when Dusty got off the shift late that night. He came into the house, took his gun belt off, and flopped down on the bed. The next morning, his wife—yeah, he was married—was getting ready to go to work when the paperboy, dressed in his rain gear, delivered The Indianapolis Star to the front porch, just when his wife was leaving. He also delivered an envelope he found tucked under the windshield wiper of the policeman's car. Inside the envelope was a note from the girlfriend, bemoaning the fact that they had an argument. Upon reading the note, the wife went into the bedroom and started hitting Dusty with his gun belt. He woke up and asked, "What's this all about?" She produced the note and told him to read it. She told him that The Star delivery boy had delivered it, and then asked him, "What are you going to do about it?" He thought a while and answered with his now-famous words: "We are canceling The Star!"

Bud and the Power Prayer

When I become state Republican Chairman, we had lots of fundraising dinners. Every dinner started with a prayer. Bud, who had started out as a beginning member of the Brothers of Holy Cross from Notre Dame, gave a great prayer. But more than just giving a great prayer, he was the only invocator I had ever heard who prayed for Republican victories while damning the Democrats. I made Bud the "Invocator for Life," a title he was very, very proud of. And sure enough, he gave every invocation at every dinner I had when I was State Chairman. I'm telling you, Bud could give a "power prayer" like nobody could. Bud is a person you would want to be in a foxhole with. He wouldn't bug-out on you. (When I ran for governor, Bud drove me. We had to change that because Bud said he couldn't see at night, and I had to drive, and Bud sat in the back. It just didn't look right.)

The Gun in the Trunk

My pal, Bud Gohmann, and his wife Vicki were driving to Marco Island, Florida to visit with us. I had a pistol in Indianapolis that I wanted to put on my Florida boat. I didn't want to go through all the required paperwork to put it in my airline baggage. I sent it with Bud. I cautioned Bud to make sure he kept it out of sight if he stopped at a motel on the way. Bud did stop and was unloading their clothes for the overnight motel stay. In the parking lot of the motel, lots of people on motorcycles pulled up beside Bud's car. According to Vicki, Bud asked, "Vicki, is the gun in the trunk?" He spelled out g-u-n and t-r-u-n-k. I guess Bud thought people who ride motorcycles can't spell. Hope no one tells Governor Mitch.

Chapter 13
Bill Hudnut

In the late '70s, with the all-time worst president—Jimmy Carter—as President, the economy took a bust. There was a gasoline shortage, the prime interest rate climbed to somewhere around 19%, there was an individual federal income tax rate of 70%, and Carter was fighting off Killer Rabbits? (I didn't understand it, either). Residential builders and land developers were taking a bath. Many hit the wall. Jim Curtis, Jim Capehart, and I had just started building Quail Run of Zionsville (an apartment project) and had borrowed a construction loan of about 3 million dollars, at prime plus 2%. We were lucky and survived.

Deercreek Golf Course and the Women's LPGA Tour

At that time, American Fletcher National Bank (AFNB) had a large loan on a condo/golf course project in Deerfield Beach, Florida. The developers were among those who defaulted on their loan, and AFNB took over the project.

Larry Hanna was president of AFNB, and he hired Tom Tuttle, who owned and ran the South Shore Country Club at Lake Wawasee, to run the project in Florida.

Ronald Reagan was elected in 1980, and the economy turned around starting in 1982.

Hanna and Tuttle also turned around Deercreek (the name of the Florida project). People were buying condos, and developers were buying tracts of undeveloped ground to build more condos.

One of the things that Hanna and Tuttle did was to get the women's LPGA tour to hold their first tournament of the year at the Deercreek Golf Course.

Being a friend of Hanna and Tuttle, I got invited to one of the, if not the first, tournaments held there.

JoAnne Carner (Big Mamma) was the Tiger Woods of the women's tour for a couple of years in the late '70s. She also lived at West Palm Beach, just a few miles from the tournament. The first day was a celebrity/pro tournament where you played with one of the pros. The format was a "scramble." I'm sure it was by luck, but our foursome included JoAnne Carner as our pro, Hanna (the president of AFNB), the CEO of one of the national corporations that was the official sponsor, and me.

Early Swings and Hits an Old Lady

Because JoAnne Carner was the year's leading tournament and money winner, and she was with us, our group was the last to tee off. There was a big crowd of spectators, probably a lot of them from West Palm Beach, the home of JoAnne. They literally lined the fairway. The PA announcer announced our foursome.

JoAnne Carner, a resident of West Palm Beach, took the tee with a mighty swing and drilled her drive 250 yards right down the middle. Next up was LarryHanna, President of AFNB, playing out of Crooked Stick Golf Course at Indianapolis, Indiana. Hanna, a single-digit handicapper, drilled it 220 yards right down the middle. The same thing with our CEO tournament sponsor, over 200 yards, right down the middle.

Next up was Rex Early, playing out of Hillcrest Country Club in Indianapolis, Indiana.

This tournament was in March, and I hadn't hit a golf ball since the last October. Also, to say the party we had the night before got a little out of hand would be an understatement. I got the tee, allowed for my left-hander's fade, took a mighty swing, and my ball dropped an old lady about 100 yards out. She went down like she had been hit with a sledge hammer.

I told my caddy, "You run over there. If I've killed her, signal to me so I can escape." Fortunately, by the time I walked over there, she was at least conscious.

As I said, the party thrown by the Indianapolis contingent the night before got a little out of hand. It was in a private dining room, and it had a fireplace. Someone thought it would be a good idea if we threw our wine glass in the fireplace like they did in the movies. We did. However, I had never seen a movie where they also threw a chair or two in the fireplace.

I do remember that the food and beverage bill was pretty salty, but the damage bill exceeded it.

Enter Mayor Hudnut

The next year, I was invited to the tournament and was to fly on a private jet owned or leased by the bank. I got a call a couple of days before we were to leave telling me that someone had dropped out, and they had invited Mayor Hudnut to take the drop-out's place.

At that time, my engineering company had several contracts with the city, and I felt if Hudnut was going, maybe I shouldn't. I felt that nobody cared what Rex Early did, but they might care about the mayor. I called the night before and let them know I had been stricken with the flu. (Thank God.) (I got a feel for those things.)

Sometime after that, there was a big investigation about the bank's running of Deercreek. Of course, the investigation was about the money and how it was spent and accounted for. This being a national bank, insured by the FDIC, the FBI became involved.

Larry Hanna lost his job and was indicted because as president of the bank, the buck stopped with him. I am sure that Larry Hanna did not personally profit from that project, but he took a hard hit.

It was ironic because Hanna and Tuttle turned a dead-loser project into a very profitable project for the bank, after it was all said and done. With all that going on (a bank president being fired), The Indianapolis Star and its investigative reporters got involved.

The Power of Rumors

The Star reporters wanted to know about the parties and who was there. They especially wanted to know about the outing that Hudnut attended.

I was asked whether there were any women around. I said that because it was a women's golf tournament, I was sure there were, and because hookers probably didn't wear name tags identifying themselves as hookers, I really didn't know whether there were any of them around. Besides that, I didn't go to the tournament the year in question. (If everybody assumed that any lady sitting alone at a bar was a hooker, a lot of guys probably got hit in the mouth by her husband after he got back from the men's room.)

It really would not have been a big deal except they knew that the mayor, former minister William Hudnut was there. Because I didn't go, I didn't know much about what Bill did or didn't' do, nor did I give a red rat's ass.

Unfortunately, my name was on the bank plane's manifest of passengers even though I had called the night before and canceled. I tell you this because I was not guilty, and besides, the statute has run out. I don't think the newspaper reporters believed me, but it happened to be true.

Rumors Keep Flying

Here is what happened later. In 1987, John Mutz, our Lt. Governor, decided to run for governor in 1988. I happen to think John would have made a great governor. He has that rare ability to totally understand politics and government. John Mutz is super-smart and is a good person. I was for John. He appointed Mike McDaniel as his campaign chairman and me as his finance chairman, and the campaign was on.

Mayor Bill Hudnut announced his interest in running for governor. As I said, John Mutz was probably one of the most-qualified men who had ever run for governor. But I have to give the devil his due. Hudnut was a charmer, and he had some County Chairman support out in the hinterlands.

What John had was the ability to communicate with the business community, and we raised a lot of money for his campaign.

Bill Cooke, from Bloomington, had a great fundraiser for John. We started early with a big fundraiser at Dawson's Lake during the summer of 1987. John raised more money than any governor's candidate had up until then. (That record has now been passed by a mile.)

At some point, Hudnut saw the writing on the wall and decided not to run. He couldn't just say something like, "I've got a great job as mayor, and I've changed my mind, and I won't be a candidate." Bill had to have an excuse. He insinuated that I had forced him out of the race. Supposedly, I had some pictures or rumors or something, connected to the trip to Florida, and because of that, Bill would get out. I heard that from several sources. So did the newspaper.

I got a call from a reporter friend of mine from The Star one day. He said the city editor had just assigned three reporters (not one, not two, but three) to investigate this.

I called Bo Conner, the Managing Editor of The Star, and asked whether I could come over to his office. I explained to him that Hudnut has used that as an escape excuse. I wasn't in Florida at the same time as Hudnut. And if I had been, I probably had better things to do than spy on Bill Hudnut. I'm a hully-gully. I ain't no voyeur. Bo said he believed me and called off the dogs.

My relationship with Hudnut was always up and down. He had the intestinal fortitude to start the Circle Centre Mall. He built the football arena without a football team, and without a clue of how to get one. (Were we lucky!)

The Hoosier Dome: Getting It Done

Bob Welch and Frank McKinney, Jr. had been lobbying the NFL for several years. I was invited to Welch's suite at the Indy 500 on one race day. His other guests were Tom Landry and the general manager of the Chicago Bears. I think they were a great help, and Welch and McKinney never got any of the credit. Nevertheless, Hudnut was like Larry the Cable Guy: "Let's get 'er done." And he did! Dave Frick, a deputy mayor, played a large role in working out many of the details.

After Hudnut announced his intentions to build the Hoosier Dome, some of our Republican City-County Councilmen and -women, and some of our legislators, were concerned about the political fallout if they voted for the dome.

Dave Frick and Hudnut asked Mike DeFabis and me to try to meet with our officeholders and convince them that they wouldn't have political problems if they voted for the dome. We were both Township Chairmen.

DeFabis and I scheduled a breakfast meeting with our officeholders and got most of their support. When the Colts came to town, I (like everyone else) entered the ticket lottery. I ended up with the worst tickets in the house. I reverted to my Crazy Indian Theory mode, reminding everyone of my involvement with the dome. Lo and behold, I got four great season tickets.

Bill had some bad publicity his last few years in office concerning his personal life. That was accelerated by The Star after he wrote his book, Minister Mayor. (Bad timing, Bill!) Regardless of that, Bill Hudnut certainly deserved better treatment from the business community and the establishment of Indianapolis.

After being elected mayor, I think Steve Goldsmith did not want to compete with Bill Hudnut's charisma. He did everything he could to make sure Bill moved on.

Tom Miller, President of Indiana National Bank, and John Hodawald of Indianapolis Power & Light tried to get Bill a meaningful job in Indianapolis. They asked me to try to get him the job as president of The Indianapolis Foundation. I tried but could not get that done. Bill would have been a really great leader of that foundation.

Love him or hate him, this city owes Bill Hudnut a great debt of gratitude.

Chapter 14
The Reagan Visit

In the 1980 election, George Bush won in Iowa. Indiana carried Reagan in the 1976 primary against President Ford, and we were going to gear up to make sure that we would carry him again in 1980.

Keith Bulen and the Reagan organization named Denny Nichols as the Reagan Chairman, Gladys Holland from Anderson was the Vice Chairman, and I was named as the Campaign Director. We were pretty confident that Reagan would win, but Bush's victory in Iowa was a wake-up call. We did do some organizing out in the counties. Usually, with us having a May primary, the ball game is over long before they get to us in May, and 1980 was no exception. It was all over but the shouting by May.

The Petitions

One of my responsibilities was making sure that we got the petitions signed and certified in each of the Congressional districts. I had been there, done that, and had a t-shirt to prove it when it came to petitions. As time went on, I got all the petitions signed and certified from every Congressional district except for the 1st District (Lake County). The County Chairman from Lake County said he would take care of it. I checked with him weekly and then daily. At last, he said he had them all, and they were certified by the clerk and in his office.

I told him that I was sending a runner to pick them up because time was running out for me to present them to the Secretary of State's office. He called back and said that someone had stolen them out of his desk. I didn't know who had committed this dastardly deed, but it happened right after he had met with John Connolly, who was also running for President and had a boatload of money.

My razor-sharp mind went to work, and I thought there might be a connection. I contacted an acquaintance of mine who had the reputation of being slicker than Brian Bosma's head. He got me the petitions. He obviously was well-organized because he got everybody to sign with the same pen. I sent Jim Buyer, from Martinsville, to get the petitions, and we got them to the Secretary of State's office on time. I doubt that Bulen would have gotten mad at me if Reagan wasn't on the Indiana ballot.

About the last week in April, Bulen asked me to pick him up at the airport and go to dinner. It seems that Bulen had gotten Reagan to come to Indianapolis.

The Fundraiser at Rex's House, Class or Not

Keith laid out plans for a big rally at the Shrine Club, and then we had time for a fundraiser. Keith asked me where we should have it. He mentioned a couple of his friends with big expensive houses. I said to Keith, "I'm his Campaign Director. I'll have it at my house". Bulen, who had a cocktail, said, "You can't have it 'cause you've got no class." After a few minutes and more cocktails, Keith agreed it was to be at my house.

I was a little late getting home that night, and I woke my wife up and said, "Guess who's coming to our house next week? Ronald and Nancy Reagan!" My own wife looked at me and said, "We can't do that. You have no class." I told her, in no uncertain terms, that was the second time I'd heard that this very night, and I was getting tired of it.

The Preparations

Getting ready for the visit was something. We had just built our house and moved in about six months earlier. My wife pointed out that our downstairs family room was adorned with an early Halloween décor. Nothing matched. She fixed that. She went to a store that sold only leather furniture. She told them who was coming and her dilemma. You ain't going to believe this, but they loaned her the furniture. When the big day came, we had a well-decorated family room while all of our furniture was stacked in the garage. We never took the furniture back, though, because she bought it all instead.

The Secret Service, Questions, and the Bathroom

The Secret Service came in the next day or so. Where were my guns? Where could Governor Reagan lay down if ill? Which bathroom could he use? There were a lot of other questions. The bathroom for the President was just inside the door that led to the pool and our backyard. I still want to install a plaque that read, "On May 4, 1980, Ronald Reagan used this bathroom." (I didn't flush it for a month.) The Reagans were there two or three hours and seemed to enjoy themselves.

Shirtless Friends Say Hello from a Boat

Some of my friends from the White River Yacht Club decided to load up a couple of pontoon boats and come up the river to our house. Our house is right on White River, and they, with no shirts but plenty of beer, yelled out, "Hello, Ronnie!" Reagan waved back. The party was great, and we all loved the Reagans.

Class, Indeed

As we walked the Reagans out to their automobile, Nancy said, "Ron, didn't you want to tell Barbara and Rex something?" He looked a little confused for a moment and then he put his hand on Barbara's shoulder and said, "I just want to tell you those people were wrong." She asked, "What people?" Reagan said, "Those people who said you didn't have any class." Everyone there got their picture taken with the Reagans. They were fun, they were kind, and they were cooperative.

Besides Governor Reagan and Nancy, there was Mike Deaver, Lynn Nofsinger, and Ed Meese, who later became Attorney General. One of my guests was my friend, Bill Ball. Now Bill is an ideologue who loves to talk. I could envision Bill talking to Reagan for the whole three hours. We assigned Ed Meese to talk to Bill, and I think he did talk to him all three hours.

It was an experience I will never forget, and I will always remember and thank Bulen for making that happen.

Some of my friends had a monument made, which is now in our backyard. It commemorates the Reagan visit.

Chapter 15
Republican State Chairman

In February 1991, I got a call from a friend. I was at our condo in Marco Island, Florida. I was playing golf, running my boat, and staying warm and happy. My friend wanted me to get back to Indianapolis and run for State Chairman. Keith Luse was chairman, and he suddenly announced that he wanted out.

I knew the party was in financial trouble, but I had no idea how bad it was. They had to move out of their office because they couldn't pay the rent. Virgil Scheidt, from Columbus, had succeeded Gordon Durnil, who had been the Chairman during the Orr administration and had chosen not to run after the 1988 loss. Virgil was a good solid Republican but was not a fundraiser. Keith Luse, a Lugar staffer, succeeded Virgil, but Luse had the same problem. He was not a fundraiser.

With a lot of urging from my wife (don't believe that), I got on a plane the next day and landed the night before the vote. I knew some of the members on the State Committee, but not all of them. John Earnest, the District and County

Chairman from Marion, was also running, and he believed that he had enough votes. I had no idea how many votes I had because I hadn't had time to do any campaigning for the job. The vote was taken, and I won by one vote. John Earnest was upset and showed it. But a couple days later, we met, and no one was more supportive or worked harder than John. We became good friends.

After the election and answering some questions from the press, I walked out in the reception area where a guy in a suit and tie wanted to see me. He was from Indiana National Bank and he wanted me to sign a note, personally guaranteeing the $300,000 the State Committee had borrowed during the waning days of the 1988 campaign. Gee. They had forgotten to tell me that or the fact that in addition to the $300,000 bank loan, we owed others someplace between $200,000 and $300,000 for a total of $500,000–$600,000. When I signed the note, I tried to insert some weasel clauses, you know, like I was not of sound mind, etc. The banker in the suit was not going to have any of that.

Prior to getting the phone call to run for State Chairman, a few weeks before, I had a meeting at my house of all the township chairmen and our County Chairman. Bill Hudnut had run his course and despite all the good things he did for the city, he collected some baggage. He was elected in 1976 and still serving in 1991. Bill had given signals he might not run. Steve Goldsmith said he was tired of being prosecutor and wanted to run for mayor. Also, Goldsmith said that if Hudnut didn't step aside, he would still not run again for prosecutor.

Paul Mannweiller, the Speaker of the House, had also told some people that he would like to be our candidate for mayor. Nobody was making any decisions, and time was running out. After some heated discussions, with the Township Chairman, we decided to encourage Hudnut to step down and we would support Goldsmith for mayor. We all shook hands and decided that was the program and that we would all support it. (I wish I had gone for Mannweiller.) I promised Goldsmith that I would co-chair his finance committee.

A few weeks later, after I became State Chairman, I called Steve and told him I was having enough trouble raising money for the party, and I couldn't help him, too. After looking at our finances, I realized I had Trouble with a capital T. I was told the next day that we didn't have the money for Friday's payroll. I called my pal, Ed French, and he sent me $5,000 for the payroll.

Also, after I was elected as chairman, I told the State Committee that I would not take a salary or expenses. That was something new. All previous chairmen had taken a salary. I also told them that I believed that people were paid for what they were worth. My pay was zero.

Tyson Trial Connection That Wasn't

One of the most bizarre things that happened to me as State Chairman was a phone call I got from the National Chairman of the Black Republicans. He wanted to come to Indianapolis and meet with me. He was a member of the Republican National Committee, as I was.

He came to my office at the appointed time and was accompanied by a lady lawyer. After some small talk, he dropped Don King's name and said he wanted to talk about Mike Tyson. King had attended a couple of our National

Committee meetings. Tyson was about to be tried for rape in an Indianapolis court.

After telling me Indiana had a reputation as a Ku Klux Klan state, he wanted to talk about the judge. He pointed out that Judge Pat Gifford was a Republican. That's when I called time-out and asked my secretary, Sheila, to come in and be a witness. I wasn't going there. I told him I wasn't going to discuss Tyson, the judge, or anybody else, and that I had to go asphalt my drive.

I figured if I had even tried to interfere with Judge Gifford, I would be getting out of the penitentiary about now. I am way too old of a cat to get screwed by kittens.

A Good, Clean Life Gets Rewarded

About two days after getting elected, I was having dinner at the country club. A friend of mine was there with his wife; and as we were leaving, he suggested I come out and see him the next day. His name was Jerry Burris, and his partner was Glenn Swisher. They owned a company called Syndicate Glass. When I went out to his office, Jerry presented me a check for $50,000, and Glen also gave me a check. Neither of them was in politics, and they didn't want anything. They just wanted me to succeed. Hallelujah. We were off and running. You see, if you live a good, clean life, you get rewarded.

Take the Money

One of the first things I did was to reinstate the vanity plate fees that the two parties got. (People who wanted their license plate to have a low number or have special lettering had to pay an extra fee. The two parties split that fee.) Keith

Luse had, for some reason, decided it was good politics to not take the money. When you can't make payroll or pay the rent, you TAKE THE MONEY. I tried to get the money that the party had turned down. When Luse decided not to take it, the money went back to the state. The State Auditor, Ann DeVore, was agreeable.

My great friend Ann DeLaney, who was the Democrat State Chairman, got an injunction against the State Auditor that prevented her from giving the Republican Party the unclaimed money it was entitled to.

After DeLaney got an injunction against the State Auditor giving us the money, I hired Dave Brooks and Murray Clark to file a lawsuit to get us the back money. Of course, DeLaney, as Democrat State Chairman, had legal representation to make sure we didn't get the back money. The law suit was taken out of Marion County. There was a list of counties compiled from which we could choose from. We struck some of the counties, and the Democrats struck some. We got down to two counties: Shelby County and Morgan County.

The Republican judge in the Shelby County court was the same judge who ruled against the Republican effort to have Evan Bayh taken off the ballot in 1988 because of the residency issue (Judge O'Connor). The leading Republican attorney in Shelby County assured Clark and Brooks that this Republican judge would be more likely to rule in our favor because he had ruled against his party in 1988 and felt bad about having to rule that way. I was reluctant to go back to this Shelby County judge, but finally said okay, upon the advice of Brooks and Clark. You guessed it: He ruled against me again.

Murray and Brooks argued who had to call me with the bad news. I must have been crazy. He got me twice.

Raising money was tough. We had a Democrat governor, Evan Bayh, and a Democrat House. In looking over the Democrat Party's financial reports, it was obvious that many of our former Republican friends were big contributors to the Democrats.

I Have to Wax My Alligator

Some would have called them whores. I just called them "fair weather friends." For instance, the lobbyist for Indiana Bell suggested that I meet with their President, Dick Nortabart. They set up a breakfast at the Columbia Club. I got there at the appointed time, and Mr. Nortabart was a little late. He sat down and asked me, "Why am I here?" One of his lobbyists said, "Mr. Nortabart, Rex Early is Chairman of the Republican Party, and we thought you ought to meet with him." He responded by saying, "We don't give money to parties."

I spoke up, "Well, you are giving to the Democrat Party!" He said, "Well, we are not donating to your party." Or words to that effect. I looked at my watch. I had been there ten minutes. And I got up and said, "I forgot, I'm supposed to be waxing my alligator, so I have got to go." And I left. He was a rude and obnoxious person. His governmental goal was to get the legislature to pass a bill legalizing measured service. He seemed to live and die with this issue. It was rumored that the next legislature might pass it. Basically your phone bill would be computed on the number of calls you made.

We were gearing up for the '92 Republican Convention. I had appointed a Platform Committee, and they had met, had hearings, and gave me the draft. I added one paragraph. "We, the Republican Party, stand with our senior citizens who depend on their phones for their well being and as such, the Republican Party stands forth right against any kind of measured service." (Or words to that effect.) How did you like those apples, Mr. Nortabart?

Hey, Mr. Nortabart, it's a long road without a turn.

George Fleetwood, who had at one time been a lobbyist, is now President of Indiana Bell and has done a great job for them.

Public Service of Indiana was also giving and raising a bunch of money for the Democrats. We got zero. I had lunch with Jim Rogers, a nice man, who was president of Public Service of Indiana. He was honest and pointed out that the Democrats controlled state government, and he had a lot of issues coming up with the Regulatory Commission, and the Democrats appointed the Commission. I didn't like it, but at least he told the truth. Jim is now president of Duke Energy.

How to Push Buttons

I had a bill drawn up that would require the voters to elect the members of the Indiana Regulatory Commission, which sets the utilities' rates. Most of the members are appointed by elected office holders. You have never seen the commotion that caused. Every utility went berserk. Senator Pat Miller carried the bill. (She had no idea what she was getting into.) The hearing of the bill was unbelievable! Every lobbyist in Indiana must have been representing someone. It turned into a lobbyist-get-rich circus.

I didn't even go to the hearing. I was just jacking with the utilities.

A Governor Not Influenced

I also met with the President of NIPSCO, the northwestern utility in Indiana. He was perfectly honest and told me he was going to be one of Evan Bayh's largest contributors. He was betting all his chips on Evan. Of course, Evan won. I did notice later on that NIPSCO had a real big case with the Regulatory Commission, and they (the commission) ruled against NIPSCO.

So much for being one of Evan's largest contributors.

By the end of the first year, I got the bank loan paid off and had negotiated or paid the rest of our debt.

The National Committee Shuffle

The National Committee men and women were elected the day before the state convention. They were Margie Hill from Bloomington, and Don Cox, the former Republican County Chairman from Evansville, who were our National Committee members. The State Chairman is also on the National Committee. Each state has three people. In 1992, I asked both Margie Hill and Don Cox to step down. Margie had been a National Committeewoman for years, and Don Cox had been on there for eight years. In most states, the National Committeeman is there because he is a good fundraiser. Cox had informed me he wasn't going to raise money for the state party. Don was not a happy camper. I replaced them with Jean Ann Harcourt, from Milroy, and Bob Hiler, from Mishawaka. Both were energetic and raised money. They also represented Indiana very well on the National Committee.

After I had stepped down, both were given important spots on the Republican National Committee. The National

Committee meetings were interesting. Lee Atwater, the Republican National Chairman, had died, and Mary Matalin was running the show on a day-to-day basis. Rich Bond was elected as National Chairman, but Mary was still in charge. I did not like Mary Matalin. She deserves James Carville.

Remember When It Ain't A-gonna Happen

The whole focus of the National Committee in 1991 and 1992 was to get George Bush elected. 1992, of course, was not a good year. We had all heard George Bush at this nomination in 1988 say, "Read my lips. No new taxes!" Well, we did get new taxes. Bush was coerced (I think) into signing a bloated budget that had to be funded with additional taxes. Ronald Reagan recognized early on that you can't please everyone. Forty to 45 percent of the electorate wouldn't vote for you if you were one of the Twelve Disciples. "It ain't a-gonna happen." Reagan realized that and didn't subvert his bedrock principles to cater to that 40 percent. George Bush, on the other hand, wanted everyone to love him, and that "ain't a-gonna happen," either.

That is a good lesson to all politicians.

In addition to the tax issue, we, the Republicans, had been in power for 12 years, and the electorate wanted a change.

I do think that George H. W. Bush was an honorable and honest man who served his country well as a fighter pilot in the war and as President of our great country.

Mrs. Bush Loves Evan

On a few occasions, the National Committee was invited to the White House. On one occasion, I was engaged in a conversation with Mrs. Bush. She read my name tag and asked, "How goes things in Indiana?" I told her that the President would carry Indiana, of course, but I really wanted to beat Evan Bayh, our governor. Mrs. Bush looked at me like I had soiled the rug at the Sistine Chapel, and said, "I love Evan Bayh! I have known him since he was a baby, and his mother was a friend of mine. In fact, he and one of my sons went to high school together and were on the basketball team. In fact, Marvella (Evan's mother) and I were sometimes the only mothers there at the basketball games."

I wanted to say, "Mrs. Bush, my name is Keith Bulen, and I just borrowed Rex Early's name tag!" I didn't want to piss off Barbara Bush.

The Chairman and the Vice President

One of the really neat things about me being on the National Committee was that Dan Quayle was Vice President. If Dan wasn't busy, he would send a staffer over to our meetings and have me come to his office. He wanted me know what was happening in politics back home and hear all the gossip. It was also a chance to see some of his staffers from Indiana. Al Hubbard was second in charge of the office, right behind Bill Crystal, who was Chief of Staff.

David McIntosh, who later was a congressman and ran for governor, was a key player on Dan's staff. Also, Bobby Bosch and Anne Hathaway played very key roles on the Vice President's staff.

Don't ever believe that Dan Quayle was not qualified to be Vice President or President, for that matter. Dan Quayle was one of the sharpest and smartest political people I ever met or will ever meet. What the press did to him was evil and unbelievable. He had been an outstanding, well-respected senator and would have made a great President.

The Perfect Candidate

The Republican State Convention in 1992 was chaotic. I invited our National Chairman to Indiana to see how a well-run party conducted its conventions. Chaos reigned supreme. Although Attorney General Linley Pearson was hard at work for four years trying to get nominated for governor, I felt he would have a hard time beating Evan Bayh.

Linley Pearson was an honorable and good man who would have made a good governor. In retrospect, I probably made a mistake not just pushing Linley. Instead, I roamed the state looking for an "all-star" who could beat Evan Bayh. As it turned out, there just wasn't such a person. Linley was not a dynamic speaker, or someone who created excitement. His worst fault, however, was that he was just God-awful with the press. 1992 was looking like a bad year nationally (and it was). And a mayonnaise-on-white-bread candidate who didn't get along with the press didn't help.

One day, I got a call from Mr. Art Decio, CEO of Skyline Corporation in Elkhart, who was a real heavy-hitter. He said he wanted me to come to his office in Elkhart as he had the perfect candidate for me to run for governor. He would send his plane to pick me up. I was excited. I couldn't wait to get there.

I was ushered into Mr. Decio's office, and my heart was pounding. "What I had been looking for!" A "secret candidate" that impressed Mr. Decio. Mr. Decio said this candidate was ready to run! We were going to beat Evan

Bayh! I almost fell out of my chair when he finally told me who his "secret candidate" was—Frank McKinney, Jr., the president of American Fletcher National Bank in Indianapolis. Certainly, Mr. McKinney was well known, and he had the money to run a campaign. The only problem was that Frank McKinney, Jr. was a Democrat! I certainly assumed he was. His father, Frank McKinney, Sr. had been the Democrat National Chairman when Harry Truman was President. (He was Murray Clark's uncle, and he was on the jet that went down in Greenwood, killing him, Bobby Welch, John Weliever, and Mike Carroll. All Indianapolis civic leaders.)

Well, I knew that "that dog won't hunt," but I can't tell Mr. Decio that it was a bad idea. I would have never been able to sell our party leaders on Mr. McKinney. Also, I didn't want to tell Mr. McKinney that. Fortunately, Beurt SerVaas was on the bank's board of directors. Beurt had Frank and me out to his office for lunch and to talk about his candidacy. Beurt and I both stressed just how time-consuming and how much hard work running for a state-wide office would be. We also stressed that you had to have a thick skin.

Frank was of the opinion that if he ran, our party people would be so grateful that he wouldn't have to do all the traveling and pressing of the flesh. A week or so later, Frank called me for a meeting with him and his wife, Mary Ann. Both agreed that Frank running for governor was not a great idea. I just couldn't see Frank McKinney at a 4-H hog-judging contest at the Decatur County Fair.

Frank would not have been a good candidate. Nobody knew that better than Frank's sister, who was Murray Clark's mother, Clara. She told me that if I took Frank as our candidate for governor, she (Murray's mom) would move out of the state of Indiana and never come back.

The "Smooth" Convention

My "all-star" candidate didn't appear, and Linley Pearson won the primary over two or three other candidates. The next step was to fill our ticket at the Republican State Convention. We had to pick a Lt. Governor, an Attorney General, and a Superintendant of Public Instruction. I had pushed Linley pretty hard to give the green light to Robert Green from Vincennes for Lt. Governor. Robert had said he could raise one-million dollars for the campaign. (I don't think that ever materialized.)

Ann DeVore, the State Auditor, had also expressed some interest in running for Lt. Governor. The party rules are pretty clear that a candidate for state office at the convention must file before noon at State Headquarters on day before the convention. Mrs. DeVore did not file.

The night before the convention, we put on a big party in any empty space outside the Indianapolis Convention Center. The rumors were flying that night that Ann DeVore and her backers didn't like the idea of Green being the Lt. Governor, and Ann would be nominated from the floor. Sure enough, when the convention was called to order, the DeVore people put on a floor demonstration. Because Green was the only candidate to file, he was going to be nominated by acclamation with a voice vote. The whole thing started to get ugly.

Now Ann, as State Auditor, was scheduled to speak. I was sitting on the front row on the aisle. Rich Bond, the Republican National Chairman, whom I had lured here to see how smooth our conventions were, sat next to me. Then Ann DeVore sat next to him. Just before Ann was to be introduced, she leaned over Rich Bond and said, "Rex Early, you don't know what I'm going to do or say, do you?" And I answered Ann, "I don't give a ret rat's ass! (or something a little stronger) what you say!"

Bond looked like he would rather have syphilis than be at our convention. He hadn't seen anything yet! When Ann spoke, she did not announce that she would run, but she did chastise me about how Green was going to be selected. (She was right. I really pushed my friend from Vincennes down Linley's throat.) Finally, Green was nominated by acclamation, but there were still some hard-liners who voted no.

Candidate Goes Berserk

Next, it was time to nominate the Attorney General. Tim Bookwalter, who is now prosecutor in Putnam County, was the winner. Linley told everybody who would listen that he would not run on the same ticket as Tim Bookwalter. Now he was just nominated, beating out Linley's candidate. Linley went berserk when the results were announced. Linley then walked out of our convention after repeating that he would not run with Tim on the ballot. The press was having a field day. Had he resigned? What was the procedure to fill the ticket? What's next? I didn't know.

Rex Puts His Foot Down

Rich Bond was trying to escape from this whole convention of crazy people. A "smooth" convention is what I had promised him. I decided we had to come to some conclusion. I asked Marge O'Laughlin to accompany me out of the convention and see whether we could find Linley. We headed for Linley's campaign headquarters a few blocks away. Sure enough, that was where he was holed up. When we got there, his entire staff was with him. I was told some wanted him to return to the convention, and some wanted him to resign as our candidate. There, giving him counsel, was Dave Miller, Sharyn Kersey, Susie Lightle, Linley's wife, Diane, and others.

After a few minutes, I announced that I was going back to the convention, and if Linley didn't want to go back with me, we would nominate a new governor's candidate at the convention. Of course, we didn't have the authority to do that, but it sounded good. Finally, Linley's wife, Diane, reminded him how hard he had worked to get the nomination, and that he should go back to the convention, Tim or not. Linley agreed, and we all went back.

A Big Mistake

Also, at the convention, we nominated Sue Ellen Reed as Superintendent of Public Instruction. She was elected in the fall and is still there. I have always counted that one of my biggest mistakes in politics, and I've had some big mistakes. I have been cringing every year when Sue Ellen Reed celebrates the fact that we are now down to only 35% of our school students who can't pass an easy test which tells how much they have learned, and how we have gone from 48th to 45th in the nation (or something like that.) Well, hu-ray! Hu-ray, let's all get a day off and celebrate! Sue Ellen is a nice lady who is opposed to accountability in our education system.

Say, "Cheese!"

Needless to say, the obligatory candidate picture was something to behold. Two of the four hated each other, and one was certainly not the choice of all the delegates. The picture reminded me of the picture you see on TV where the Palestinians are meeting with the Israelis. After the picture, Rich Bond said he had to hurry back to Washington and mumbled about our "Chinese fire drill." Needless to say, Rich Bond didn't put me on any of the good committees. I guess he couldn't take a joke.

State Election Results

Linley got beat for governor by Evan Bayh. Bookwalter lost the Attorney General election. But Sue Ellen Reed, with $65,000 the party had given her, beat Stan Jones for Superintendant of Public Instruction. We won a congressional seat we were supposed to lose. Steve Buyer, just back from Desert Storm, was elected to Congress, beating Democrat Jim Jontz.

We also elected Dan Coats to his first six-year term after being appointed by the governor to take Dan Quayle's seat and having won a two-year term in 1990.

The New Republican National Chairman

After Bush lost in 1992, we had our Republican National Committee election to elect a new National Chairman. We met in St. Louis. Dan Quayle was on the phone, asking me to support Spence Abraham from Michigan. He also had the support of Betsy DeVoss, the wife of the Amway president. She didn't speak to me after I didn't vote for Spence. Come to think of it, she didn't speak to me before the vote.

John Ashcroft, a senator who would later be George W.'s Attorney General, had a lot of support. But my favorite was Haley Barbour. Mitch Daniels called me and asked for my support for Haley. There were also two or three other candidates, all of which had some support.

Indiana, like the rest of the states, had three votes. Bob Hiler, our National Committeeman, had promised Dan Quayle he would go for Spence Abraham. Jean Ann Harcourt, our Committeewoman, had promised her first vote to Abraham, but would vote with me for Barbor on the second ballot. She did that. I stayed with Haley through all the ballots, and he won. Haley is now the governor of Mississippi, and is being mentioned as a candidate for Vice President.

I was for Haley because I thought with a Democrat President, Bill Clinton, we needed a colorful spokesman for the party, and Haley was certainly that. I served on the National Committee with Haley. I had first met him when he was assistant for Mitch Daniels when Mitch was Reagan's political director.

Two Hoosiers, Bipartisanship, Toyota, and a Lot of New Jobs

I got a call from my good friend from Evansville, Bob Ossenberg. Bob and a lawyer from Princeton, Indiana, named George Rehnquist, had been trying for months to get Toyota to locate a plant in southwest Indiana. George led the charge, and Bob worked on the Evansville contingency for their support. Bob's call was made in desperation. Toyota had basically agreed to locate at a site near Princeton but was getting no encouragement from the governor's office.

In fact, they had heard rumors that the Toyota plant, if located in Indiana, would become a "political football" in the upcoming election for the United States Senate. Evan had made it pretty clear that with his term running out, he would be a candidate for the United States Senate and oppose Dan Coats for the seat.

Now Evan had used the Subaru plant in Lafayette to beat John Mutz. John, as Lt. Governor, had worked very hard to bring the Subaru plant and the new jobs to Indiana. Every Legion and VFW Club heard Evan's criticism of Mutz for bringing a Japanese plant to Indiana. According to Evan, it was downright unpatriotic. As State Chairman, I had been on him about his Highway Department buying Japanese tractors instead of good old Massey Fergusons and John Deeres.

Evan was in a box if he pushed for Toyota. He was afraid that Senator Coats would be all over him about being disingenuous and a flip-flopper.

Coats, on the other hand, was concerned that if he endorsed Toyota coming to Indiana, Evan would do the same thing to him that he had done to Mutz. What we had was a "Chinese stand-off."

According to Ossenberg, Toyota would not locate here and be the subject of a political fight. They would go to another site they liked in Tennessee. Time was running out. To think that depressed, southwestern Indiana was going to lose all those jobs because of politics was unacceptable.

I called Coats and asked him whether he would get on-board if Evan would, and he agreed. I called Ed Lewis and got the same agreement from Evan: that if Coats agreed, Evan would, too.

I called back to Ossenberg and told him that he could

report both Evan and Dan Coats would be supportive, and they were. In fact, Evan played a role in Toyota's formal announcement. Dan Coats decided he didn't want to run again. Southwestern Indiana got a great asset with lots of new jobs.

Someplace in southwestern Indiana there ought to be a statue of George Rehnquist. He was the guy that wouldn't give up. Also, his cohort from Evansville, Bob Ossenberg, should be honored.

George was the Economic Development Chairman from Gibson County. Bob Ossenberg was just a volunteer from Evansville trying to help their economy. They had no budget, no airplane trips to Japan, and no publicity directors, and no fanfare. They were just two Hoosiers who worked hard and delivered. Hey, governor, how about a Sagamore of the Wabash for both of them? It is a little late, but they certainly deserved it. One of the few Sagamores I am aware that Mitch has given out went to one of his Ivy Tech Board appointments who voted against Mitch's choice for President of Ivy Tech.

Early Meets Starr

When Dan Coats was appointed the U.S. Ambassador to Germany, I was invited to a small reception in Washington, DC.

Among the guests were Senator Joe Lieberman, Senator Elizabeth Dole, Bob Dole, and some others I had read about or had seen on TV.

I noticed this one little guy standing alone by the food table. He looked like a lost soul. And he looked so familiar that I was sure that I knew him. I also knew he wasn't a senator or high-profile congressman.

I finally figured out he was from Vincennes, but I just couldn't think of his name. Finally, I couldn't stand it anymore. So, I walked over and asked him, "Ain't you from Vincennes?" He replied, "My name is Ken Starr." I said, "My name is Country Bumpkin, and I'm sure glad to meet you."

Leaving on Top

In February, it was time to elect the State Chairman. I had announced far and wide that I was through. Two years were enough. Even though 1992 was not a good year for Republicans nationally (George Bush lost to Clinton), our party in Indiana was alive and well. We carried George Bush in Indiana; we elected a brand-new congressman, Steve Buyer, who was just back from duty in Desert Storm; and lo and behold, we elected Sue Ellen Reed as Superintendant of Public Education. I took over the party with close to $600,000 in debt. I left with all the bills paid and one million dollars in the bank. We had a new computer system in headquarters, paid for, and a voter name list that was correct. (That was an all-time first!) And I had worked two years, full time, without a salary or expenses. I was also proud of recruiting my pal, Bud Gohmann, because he was the only person who actually prayed for Republicans to win and prayed for the defeat of Democrats.

I owed a lot to Devon Anderson, my Chief of Staff and right hand, who knew what we needed in the way of computers. (I'm computer-illiterate.) He also understood campaign finance laws and kept us out of trouble in that area. He also knew how to leverage "clean money" that the federal campaigns needed, and who would give you two-to-one dollars of "dirty" money (corporate donations). Also, my assistant, Sheila Mawrey, was a great help along with my Vice Chairman, Shirley Baker.

When I left, we also had a party that had regained its spirit and was set to win. And win they did (big time) in 1994. Nevertheless, Senator Borst, in his book Gentlemen, It's Been My Pleasure, called me a divisive State Chairman. I guess if you disagreed with him, or anything, it was "divisive."

Finding the Right New Guy

When it was known I was leaving, I got a call from Al Hubbard, who was the Number Two man on the Vice President's staff. He wanted to be State Chairman, but he readily admitted he didn't know any of the State Committee members. I felt I owed John Earnest (who I had run against) some consideration. I also felt that Mike McDaniel, who wanted the job, should also be considered. Nevertheless, I violated my own rule about not trading old friends for new ones and supported Al Hubbard because I knew Hubbard could raise money. If we had a Republican governor, I would have supported Earnest or McDaniel because money is a lot easier to raise when you have the governor. But when I was leaving, we had a Democrat governor, Evan Bayh, and Republican money was tight. Hubbard was somewhat of a hard-sell to the committee, but I finally convinced them they needed someone who could raise money. Hubbard was elected.

The Punishment of Silence

Now, at my age, I know that "no good deed goes unpunished," but I did expect at least a phone call that Al was going to work for Goldsmith for governor. Especially since he had suggested I run because I could bring the "Reagan independents" and Democrats back home. I read that Al was working for the Goldsmith campaign in the newspaper.

I guess it was no surprise to me that Al Hubbard was one of the first Hoosiers to come out for George W. Bush. At that time, Dan Quayle was testing the waters as he wanted to run. I realize that Al was the Number Two man on Quayle's Vice Presidential staff, but it looked like Bush was the favorite to win. Al became one of George W's top domestic advisors. In all deference to Al, he had gone to college with George W., and they had been friends, but it was Quayle who brought Hubbard to the dance, and you dance with who brung you.

Sometimes Water Is Thicker Than Blood

The other important person to come out early for George W. was Steve Goldsmith. This was hard for me to figure out because Dan Quayle and Steve Goldsmith's wife were first cousins. Dan Quayle's mother and Margaret Goldsmith's mother were sisters. Eugene Pulliam, the publisher of The Indianapolis Star, was their grandfather. Besides that relationship, Quayle's wife had been Steve Goldsmith's co-chairman when he ran for governor against me. I would have liked to have been at the first family reunion after Goldsmith's endorsement. It proves that sometimes, water is thicker than blood. I'm going to try to find out whether the Quayles and the Goldsmiths exchange Christmas gifts or go to family reunions.

The Politics of People

I came out early for George W. only because the Quayles didn't support me, and I was miffed. I was invited to Austin, Texas, to have lunch with George W. I went, and there were about five or six people there from other parts of the country. I sat next to George W. at lunch and found him to be a very likeable person. A guy you wouldn't mind going hunting or fishing with. (I am very disappointed with our President on his immigration policy and the run-away spending that has occurred on his watch.)

Back home in Indiana, if Dan Quayle couldn't have the support of a former Indiana State Republican Chairman and top staffer, Al Hubbard; the mayor of Indianapolis and his wife's cousin, Steve Goldsmith; and a hully-gully politician who had been State Chairman (me), Quayle was in trouble. He soon dropped out.

One Smart Hoosier

I made a mistake in not endorsing Dan. (Not that it would have done any good.) He would have made a good President. Despite what the national press did to Dan Quayle, he was very well qualified. So he thought the people in Latin American spoke Latin. So did I.

He was smart, and he had good Hoosier common sense. As far as Hubbard and Goldsmith, I ain't sure I would want to share a foxhole with them, but, of course, neither one of them had ever seen a foxhole. They weren't so dumb. They both supported the winner. Hubbard got a job in the White House, and Goldsmith has made a lot of contacts the last eight years.

The Republican Clinton Connection

There was more controversy as I was leaving office that involved Paul Helmke, the mayor of Fort Wayne and later a candidate for the U.S. Senate on the Republican ticket. Helmke was a classmate of Bill and Hillary Clinton at Yale. They have remained friends ever since college days. President Clinton proposed legislation (a stimulus package) that involved a tax increase. All of our Republican Congressmen, as well as Senator Lugar, were opposed to it. As Mayor of Fort Wayne, Paul wiggled a chance to testify about this bill at a Senate committee hearing. I am sure everyone thought that Republican Mayor Helmke would speak against it. Wrong. He was a proponent of the legislation. The Indiana Policy Review named him "Remocrat of the Year." Helmke now heads up an organization promoting "gun control."

As State Chairman, I wrote a rather blistering letter to Helmke about his testimony. Some way, the Fort Wayne papers got a copy of my letter. (It could have been because I sent them a copy.) It made a front page story. Helmke, of course, was upset about my letter.

Later on, Paul was running for re-election as mayor. Steve Shine, the Allen County Chairman, called and asked whether I would come to Fort Wayne and endorse Helmke. That would show all was forgiven between us, especially when the TV and newspaper people would see me giving Helmke a contribution. Shine told me that if I would do that, he and Paul would be supportive of my campaign. That was certainly my understanding, but that never happened. I carried Allen County without their help.

Props

Despite my personal differences with Al Hubbard, he was a good State Chairman. He could and did raise a lot of money. In fact, he raised the level of giving dramatically. I had lots of contributors in the $1,000–$2,000 area. Al was fearless; he would ask for $5,000 and $10,000 dollars. Al later went to work in the White House as President George W. Bush's economic advisor, and we all know how good our economy is now in 2008. Great job, Al.

Mike McDaniel was also a good State Chairman. He loved the job and was cut out to be a State Chairman. He was a great organizer and spent a lot of his blood sugar and effort in raising money the old-fashioned way: putting together state fundraising dinners with a top-notch main speaker. He had all the well known speakers, and he seemed to really like serving on the National Committee. Mike really wanted the Republican National Convention to be in Indianapolis, and almost got it.

Mike was still a believer in the grass-roots efforts. No one has ever loved the job like Mike did.

Jim Kittle worked hard on the McIntosh campaign for governor and got the bug to get totally involved. I supported John Earnest against him because I felt I owed John for all his effort when I was chairman and also when I was a candidate. Kittle won fair and square.

If Hubbard had no problem asking Republican donors for big contributions, Kittle exceeded that. He was totally fearless in asking. Jim was a great fundraiser. He also put his heart and soul into the job.

His helping Carl Brizzi to be the Marion County

Prosecutor with state party money took both imagination and guts. (Only two of 18 members of the State Committee are from Indianapolis.) He also was way out in front of the Mitch Daniels for governor effort. He was the first State Chairman to help elect a Republican governor in 16 years.

Murray Clark was my candidate for governor in 2004. If Mitch had not decided to run, I feel sure that Murray would have been nominated and elected. Mitch made a good choice when he asked Murray to be the State Chairman. Everyone who knows him likes Murray Clark, especially out in the grass-roots hustings.

Being State Chairman with a governor and being State Chairman without a governor is the difference between ice cream and dog poop. The governor is the titular head of the party. Pure and simple, the State Chairman supports his governor. It is easier to raise money if you have the governor, but that's only true if the governor will help you. (People want to contribute to the governor, not to the party, unless the governor lets it be known he wants contributors to be supportive of his party.)

Murray has been a great spokesman in publicly pushing the governor's agenda and answering any criticism from the Democrats. He is the perfect State Chairman with Mitch Daniels as governor. He looks good on TV, and he is very articulate.

In the primary election of 2000, David McIntosh was nominated for governor. The Republican State Convention nominated Murray Clark as Lt. Governor. Murray was a state senator, but he wasn't well known throughout the rest of the state.

In a Car with Marines and Their Music

Murray asked me to accompany him and help him meet some of my friends and supporters in southwest Indiana. Especially, he wanted to meet those County Chairmen and the Vice Chairmen that he didn't know. Murray's father, Jim, went with us. Jim Clark and I served in the Indiana Legislature together.

I drove my car, and therefore, we got to play my CD of Marine Corps music. Jim Clark served in the Marine Corps as an officer and was in Korea during the Korean War. Jim and I loved the music and played the CD more than once. Murray was not impressed. Also, the acoustics in my SUV were probably bad because with me driving and Jim in the back seat, Murray said the two of us asked, "HUH?" several hundred times during the trip. Murray intimated that Jim and I had a hearing problem. He also asked me whether I had other CDs that didn't play the Marine Corps Hymn. Jim and I both had our feelings hurt about the rejection of our music and the insinuation that we couldn't hear well.

How Many Ears of Corn?

On the way back to Indianapolis, I pointed out that Murray, if elected Lt. Governor, would be in charge of the Department of Agriculture. While riding through some great southern Indiana farmland, I asked Murray whether he knew how many ears of corn were on a single stalk. I figured the head of agriculture should know that. He said he wasn't real sure. I asked him to guess. Murray guessed eight ears to a stalk, and his father Jim thought it was only five.

We happened to be driving down a road with corn fields

on both sides, so I pulled off the road and drove right to the edge of a corn field. It was August, and the stalks were tall. I made them get out and look. Any dumb ass knows that there is only one ear per stalk, and Murray Clark was going to be in charge of agriculture?

A week later, back in my office, there was a pitiful looking corn stalk on my desk with two "midget" ears on it. I'm sure Murray placed it there. (Yeah, I know today there are hybrids out that produce more than one ear.)

I can honestly say that being State Chairman was the most fun I ever had with all my clothes on. It's a lot more fun if you don't have the governor's office. You don't have to answer to anyone. Harder to raise money, but more fun!

Chapter 16
Indiana Week in Review

It was fun.

The Beginning

I was the Republican State Chairman in 1991. Jim Shella, the State House and political reporter for WISH Channel 8, was putting together a TV show to air on WFYI, the local public television station. He called and asked whether I wanted to be one of the participants.

Does a hog love slop?

Does a tornado like a trailer camp?

Is a 15-pound robin fat?

Of course, I wanted to be on his show.

I always liked the McLaughlin Report, where that goofy Eleanor Clift and Pat Buchannan would argue with each other and everyone talked at once. Jim, whose show it was, liked a more sane discussion of the issues without insulting each other.

Jim is a great guy and a friend, so he certainly could dictate how he wants the show to be run. I just like arguing. I must like it. I'm married, aren't I? Now my number-one target for arguing was Ann DeLaney, who was the Democrat State Chairman when Jim started the show.

In addition to Ann, there was Sue (Emerson) Dillman, who was an Indianapolis reporter for the South Bend paper, and Jon Schwantes, who was then a reporter for The Indianapolis News. Some of the substitutes were Democrats Bill Mareau (also known as Bill Monroe) and Robin Winston (also known as Robert Winston). If you call people the wrong name on TV, it upsets them.

Men and That New Leather Smell

Now as I said, Ann was fun to argue with because she was usually wrong but always sure of herself. One time, Ann showed up for the show with a brand-new leather jacket and skirt. Just before we went on, I asked her whether she knew why men liked women to wear leather skirts. She said no. I told her, "So they smell like new cars." She just looked at me with amazement.

That Early Got a Few Calls and Letters

Once in awhile, I think I irritated the PBS TV man in charge of our show. We were talking about the Iraq-Iran war. They had killed a million or so people on each side. I asked, "Who cares?" The TV station got calls and letters about my comment. Some viewers thought that was a little crass. We had several discussions about gays in the military. I had some strong feelings about that, and I was told there were some calls and letters criticizing my stand on the issue.

One of our substitutes often on the program was the IUPUI professor, Brian Vargus. He was also a pollster. In

1994, Vargus predicted a clear Democrat sweep of the competitive congressional contests. The Republicans won, and I stuck it to Vargus pretty hard. I told him not only could he not pick the congressional winners, but that "he was so bad he couldn't pick his daddy out of a roomful of Chinamen." I think they got some calls on that; probably from Chinamen.

Franklin College and a Quayle Tangent

We appeared before numerous organizations whose program was the Indiana Week in Review crew discussing the issues of the day, complete with a question-and-answer time.

One of the most memorable was at Franklin College where they had a large crowd for their yearly meeting, that started early with cocktails. After a lengthy dinner with several speakers, we were finally on. By then, everyone was tired.

Just Ann, Jim, and I were there, and our chemistry was not working well. Ann got off on a tangent about how terrible and dumb our Vice President, Dan Quayle, was. I think she had forgotten that the Pulliam family was a big benefactor of Franklin College—and, of course, Dan Quayle's mother was a Pulliam. We went over like a lead balloon. That was the most we ever got paid for a program, and I was glad we got our money first.

Early's Ray Charles Moment

One of my most embarrassing moments was a program we put on for some organization that was involved with disabled people. Some of the disabled people at the luncheon were vision-impaired. Ann and I were arguing, and I was trying to point out something that I thought was obvious. I said, "Ann, even Ray Charles could see that." I am sure I offended some people there, and I didn't mean to.

Early Serenades DeLaney

One segment that was memorable was when young John Dillon was the head of the Department of Transportation for the Evan Bayh administration. Now Dillon had bought several Kubota tractors for use by the Highway Department. No big deal except that Evan Bayh, in his run for governor, made a big issue about John Mutz. John, as Indiana Lt. Governor, helped bring the Subaru automobile plant to Lafayette. It was our state's first Japanese plant, and Evan was against it. His campaign had stirred up some of the American Legion and VFW people about dealing with the Japanese. Now his Highway Department was buying Japanese tractors. I was giving Ann hell about her governor's flip-flop. She was defending his action.

While arguing with her, I remembered a Japanese song I learned while stationed in Japan when I was in the Marine Corps. I didn't know what the Japanese words meant, but I sang it to her on TV. She looked at me like I was insane. She was so shocked she shut up for a minute or two. I think it was Japanese love song.

Ann is really kind-hearted and a good person. Her great work with The Julian Center, a shelter for battered women, is recognized all over the state.

Even with that, Ann is usually dead wrong about the issues, and she knows I'm always right. And she still needs a check-up from the neck up.

Chapter 17
The Governor's Race

One day in 1995, I lost my mind and decided I would run for governor. Surely the butter had slipped off my biscuit.

I had been the Republican State Chairman for two years and represented the Republican Party on Indiana Week in Review for over five years. I figured I had some, not much, but some name recognition. Evan Bayh couldn't run again, so it was an open seat.

Dan Quayle had gone down with George Bush in 1992. Dan still had aspirations to be President. He ran well as a senator in Indiana, and there were those who thought his easiest way to the White House would be after he was Governor of Indiana. He would have been a good governor. He was smart, and he had good Hoosier common sense. Steve Goldsmith was also talking about running, but that was not definite.

The Butter Slipped off the Biscuit

I started floating around the governor idea. One of the

people who thought that was a good idea at the time was Al Hubbard, who succeeded me as State Chairman. Hubbard thought that I could "get back" our independents and those Democrats who voted for Reagan in '80 and '84. I had told the press and others that if Dan Quayle ran, I would not. With Dan's name recognition and his experience, it would be just a waste of time, and I knew it.

A member of the press asked whether I would run for governor if Dan's wife, Marilyn, ran. (A rumor someone started.) I said I would probably run if she ran. That was a mistake. I think this made her really mad. Dan jacked around, saying he hadn't made up his mind for a good while. But finally, with people telling him that being governor of Indiana was beneath him, he said he would not run.

I went full blast. I felt that Goldsmith had to decide whether to file for mayor of Indianapolis again (in 1995) or skip that and file for governor. I didn't think he would do both—file for four more years as mayor and also run for governor. I was mistaken. The first thing I did while Goldsmith was running for mayor was to get commitments from as many Republican County Chairmen as I could. I got around 70 out of 92 counties to endorse me. If we had been running for a convention instead of a primary, it would have been no contest. I thought that kind of early support from the county chairmen would scare off Goldsmith. I heard that at one time Goldsmith wavered, but he didn't break.

In addition to Goldsmith, Senator Bob Garton, Pat Rooney, and George Witwer also ran and tried to garner support. Garton and Rooney both dropped out. Garton couldn't raise money, and Rooney couldn't get any support. George Witwer stayed in. In the meantime, Goldsmith was fortunate that the Democrats did not run a well-financed contender for mayor. The Democrats nominated Z. Mae Jimison, a lady judge, who with no money, ran a lot closer to Goldsmith than he or his backers ever suspected.

Our primary race was a classic race. I ran a people/grass-roots campaign. That campaign will probably be the last state-wide, grass-roots campaign. In the 2004 race, Governor Mitch Daniels went to the grass-roots areas, but he was able to back up his campaign with plenty of money to buy all the media he needed.

Goldsmith ran a well-financed media campaign although he or his representatives made most of the mandatory campaign gatherings. Steve was famous for "pulling an Elvis" at most of the dinners. After he spoke, just like Elvis, Steve had "left the building." He gave the impression he would rather have a root canal than have to stick around, shake hands, and make small talk with the locals. There were times when he made Bobby Knight look nice and polite. I loved the shaking hands and socializing after the dinners.

As I wrote before, party primaries are name ID contests, and Steve had 12 years as the Marion County Prosecutor and five years as mayor. He had been on Indianapolis TV and radio constantly. The Indianapolis media market reaches an inordinate amount of Republican primary voters. There was really no difference in our stands on the issues. Less government, more privatization, lower property taxes, pro-life, etc. My big deal was a $25 license plate. At that time, you paid an excise tax when you got your license plates. The more expensive cars were taxed from $800 to $1,000 for a license plate. Mine was a popular stand.

The White River Yacht Club and Those Plates

My friends at the White River Yacht Club had a fund-raiser for me. I was giving my impression of a Bill Jenner speech and was talking about my $25-license plate idea. I got a great reception when I mentioned it. Knowing that most of my White River pals drove pickup trucks, I threw in a $15-license plate on pickups. The place went wild. To put the icing on the cake, I said that if they had a God, Guns, and Guts bumper sticker on their pickup, it would only be $5. I picked up the whole crowd.

That year, riverboat casino licenses were being handed out with a pretty hefty tax on their gross. Senator Borst and the legislature ear-marked some of the tax money the state would receive from the riverboats, directing that money to take the place of most of the license plate tax. They destroyed that issue. The right-to-life issue seemed to be the overriding issue. Even though everyone running supported right-to-life, it became a contest of who was the more right-to-life. I had John Price and Jim Bopp working hard for me. Both were social conservatives with state-wide contacts. Goldsmith had Eric Miller working the state for him.

A Note about Loyalty

When John Price ran for senator, and governor after that, I supported him both times. He was my pal. I was delighted when Jim Bopp became National Committeeman after Mitch was elected. I assume that Goldsmith, in recognition of Eric Miller's help in his campaign, supported Eric Miller for governor instead of Mitch. After all, that would be the right thing for Steve to do. For the life of me, I cannot remember reading or hearing where Steve was supporting Miller.

The Earlys—Gertrude - Rex - Henry

High school football teammates

Oakland City, Indiana—Jr. Legion Team

Rex Early
Only wusses wear face guards

Rex and Barbara Early
-Wedding day-

Parris Island - Boot Camp - Graduation day

M.P. Camp Lejeune

Working in the rice fields

REX EARLY, U.S.M.C.

Going overseas on the USS Montrose

Charlie Company - Fuji, Japan

Charlie Co. - 1st Battalion - 3rd Marines, November 1955
South Camp - Fuji, Japan

Two turkeys (one is dead)

To Rex Early — with appreciation for his friendship and support — and best wishes always —
Bill Hudnut

Great Grandfather Col. Robert Fagg
A Confederate Soldier

Never mind the key, how about an engineering contract?

The day that Dick Lugar and I decided which one of us would be the better senator

From L to R: Unknown - Bob Dole's daughter - Rex Early - Bob Dole

Announcement for Governor day

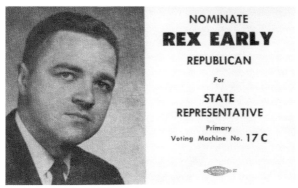

1962 Primary Election
(I won - I won)

Vincennes University Graduation
Governor Evan Bayh received an Honorary Doctorate

Right after I told George not to say
"Read my lips—no new taxes"
unless he meant it.

The day I advised Jim Shella to
quit selling used cars and try
to get a job with a T.V. station.

From L to R: Barbara Early - Nancy Reagan - President Ronald Reagan - Rex Early

From L to R: Rex Early - President Ronald Reagan - Barbara Early - Nancy Reagan
Why is Barbara giggling?

From L to R: Angela Early Schroeder - Nancy Reagan
President Ronald Reagan - Patrick Early

From L to R: Nancy Reagan - President Ronald Reagan - Mike Early

From L to R: Keith Bulen - President Ronald Reagan - Rex Early - Nancy Reagan
I was advising him to use the line - "Tear down that wall, Mr. Gorbachaf."
He said he would consider it.

From L to R: Indiana Governor Mitch Daniels and Rex Early

About to give the count for Indiana
at the 1992 National Convention
(How about all my badges?)

The Indiana Republican
State Convention

George McGovern and Rex Early
Two "has-beens"

The marker in France where a nurse
from Indiana was laid to rest

*Right after Mike McDaniel and I told Karl Rove
to blame everything on Scooter Libby*

The charming Ann DeLaney and Rex Early

Newt Gingrich - My first choice for President in 2008

With Vice President Quayle on Air Force Two

My loyal and great staff when I ran for Governor
relaxing at Marco Island after the primary election

Henry Kissinger thanking me for the advice
I gave him about foreign relations

Jack Hesseldenz (partly blocked), Rex Early,
and The General-Jack Dillon

Jug Eckert and Rex training for the Z's Pub track meet

From L to R: Murray Clark - James Kittle - Mike McDaniel - Rex Early
Indiana Republican Party Chairmen

Ref -
When do we take this show on the road -
Dan Q---

Dan Quayle and Rex Early

The current Rex Early family with the insert
Top row L to R: Rick Schroeder - Lindsay Schroeder - Rex
Mike Early - Bart Early - Pat Early
Bottom row L to R: Emily Schroeder - Angie Schroeder - Barbara Early
Lisa Early - Kirstine Early - Bailee Early - Erica Early - Shaela Early - Kianna Early

The big screen at the 1992 Republican National Convention
Who's the fat guy?

The Mayor Who Ran for Governor

Steve did what I hoped he would not do. He ran for mayor and won, and immediately ran for governor. Now Steve's run for governor had a couple of little boosts that helped him. The first one was that his wife, Margaret, was a Pulliam. Margaret's grandfather was Eugene Pulliam, the patriarch of the family. Also, he was the owner and publisher of The Indianapolis Star and The Indianapolis News. I felt their reporting of the campaign was, at times, one sided. (I might have been paranoid.) Margaret and the managing editor, Frank Caperton, were close, and it showed. I do think that Mary Beth Schnieder, who is a knowledgeable and fair reporter, and Kathleen Johnson (who left soon after the campaign) both were fair. But it's tough when the editor is talking to your opponent's wife.

The NYC Murder-Rate Spot Was True

Steve had been a good prosecutor, but I still had to take a shot at him. (You have to boil the hog to get any lard.) One of the top officers of the Indianapolis Police Department slipped me an FBI report that showed that New York City had a lower homicide rate per citizen than Indianapolis. Rudy Giuliani was Mayor of New York City, and he had been able to reduce the crime rate. We did a 30-second TV spot comparing the New York City/Indianapolis homicide rate. According to FBI statistics, there were more homicides per citizen in Indianapolis than in New York. Well, you would have thought I was a stupid Benedict Arnold. There was no doubt in the newspaper's mind that I was a gross ignoramus. (That is 144 times worse than an ordinary ignoramus!) That TV spot cost me votes.

Several months after the election, the FBI report was reported in the newspaper. One of the reporters in the Behind Closed Doors section of The Star wrote a small column that stated, "Rex was right." I understand the writer was called in and chastised by the editor.

Many years ago, under the Bob Early and Bo Conner regime, The Indianapolis Star would run a little questionnaire that asked, "Was it fair? Was it factual?" You could fill it out and send it in if you had a complaint. They quit that too soon. They were both great men who kept government honest and above board for many years. You did not want them and Dick Cady on your case.

I really don't have any hard feelings about Margaret doing everything she could to support her husband. Blood is thicker than water (although five years later, Steve supported George Bush for President, instead of Margaret's first cousin, Dan Quayle). Somewhat of a surprise was the vote in Lake County. I had some good supporters in Crown Point and some of the smaller Republican communities in Lake County.

I heard later that one of Goldsmith's myrmidons, who did a lot of business with the Goldsmith administration, was close to one of Bob Pastrick's sons. Did Pastrick help Goldsmith? I don't know: Bob Pastrick has been the King of Democratic Politicians. In any event, I lost heavy in the normal Democratic areas.

Chicken and a Blown Fuse

The campaign was fun. I traveled to every county. I ate enough chicken to make Colonel Sanders take note. We drove in snow and ice. Our car broke down on the Indiana

Toll Road. And I flew in airplanes with pilots you wouldn't believe. I was flying in a small plane one night, and the door came open. Another time, we flew at night, and our instrument light blew a fuse. I had to hold a flashlight with a weak battery from New Albany to Terre Haute. My pilot was a former jet-jockey in Vietnam, and he thought that was funny.

He's One of Us

Our campaign motto was, "He's one of us." That was meant to portray me as an ordinary person— someone who grew up poor, worked hard, and would govern with the same values as the average Hoosier. We had "He's one of us" on our brochure. Someone even bought several cartons of coffee cups with the motto printed on the side to be given away. I got a call from an attorney. It seems that someone from the Jewish organization, B'nai B'rith, had construed this to be anti-Jewish because at times, Steve Goldsmith was Jewish. I tried to explain what it really meant. Then the NAACP called and said it meant I was anti black. I even got a call from the Log Cabin Republicans asking whether that meant I was one of them. (That's the gay Republicans organization.) Several years after the election, my wife had a garage sale. She had a case of those coffee cups for fifty cents. She didn't sell one.

And He Won't Drop the Ball

I think one of the mistakes I made was when Jim Harbaugh, the quarterback for the Colts, wanted to do a commercial for me. It was right after the Colts almost made the Super Bowl on a Hail-Mary pass that our receiver (we discovered after un-piling the bodies) had dropped. Harbaugh envisioned using the TV clip, and then when they moved all the bodies, I'd be on the bottom with the ball. The voiceover would then say, "Rex Early won't drop the ball." Why didn't I do that?

The Loyal Campaign Committee

I had a great campaign committee. My chairman, Dick Freeland from Fort Wayne, one of Indiana's great people, went from a ironworker to become one of Indiana's most successful businessmen. The co-chairmen were Congressman Steve Buyer and Congressman Danny Burton. Both knew I was the underdog, but both had the guts to get on board with me. John Sweezey and other great friends were in Switzerland; they were neutral. Did I think that John Price, with little or no money, could beat David McIntosh for governor? I don't think so. Sometimes, loyalty is more important than winning. I worked for Price.

The Great Early Staff

Policy Committee
    Dick Freeland – Fort Wayne
    Mike Young – Indianapolis
    Jim Bopp – Terre Haute
    Jean Ann Harcourt – Milroy
    John Zentz – Bremen
    John Earnest – Muncie
    Billy Rendell – Peru

Campaign Committee
Mike Young – Campaign Manager
Jean Grandstiff – Scheduler, office manager
Kevin Eck – Political Director
Alex Carroll – I.T. guy
Ryan Magnus – Jack of all trades
Jackie Carroll – Alex's sister helped with computer and
Jill of all trades
Shawn McCarthy – Campaign Finance Director
Amy Walsh – Campaign Finance
Russ Semnick – Media Director
Jerry Baker – Grassroots Political Director
Sharyn Kersey and Susie Lightle – Grassroots, both
active in the Republican Women's Federation
Linda Rusthoven – Campaign Treasurer
Peter Rusthoven – Consultant

The Advisor Who Wasn't

I got a call from Dick Morris, the former Bill Clinton advisor, turned Republican, and now a regular on the Fox News Channel. He was a friend of my TV consultant, Stuart Stevens, and wanted to meet with me. I first met him when he worked on the Dan Coats senatorial campaign. He flew into Indianapolis, and we met at a Holiday Inn. He had no intention of joining the campaign. He wanted to be my "idea consultant." He also wanted a hefty monthly fee. He said he would give me a "freebie" that was working in a California race. The freebie was affirmative action. I used it in a couple of my next speeches, and the people from Jasper and Greensburg and Putnam County thought I was talking in some foreign language. Why did they care if I was against affirmative action if they didn't have a clue how it affected them?

It's About the Money

I would rather have a root canal than keep asking my friends for money. It is the worst thing a candidate has to do, and it has driven a lot of good people out of running or holding office. Because our political parties no longer have conventions, primaries are all about money. I truly believe I could nominate John Wayne Gacy if I had enough money. In the fall, we have enough straight-party voters that money is not quite as important as in the primary. This is especially true in state-wide races where most of the electorate just don't know much about the candidates.

In 1996, the five candidates for the Republican governor's nomination collected and spent 12 million dollars. Steve Goldsmith spent $7.5 million; I spent $3 million; and Rooney, Witwer, and Garton spent close to $2 million, most of it coming from Rooney. Contrast this with the fact that the first million-dollar campaign in this state was the Bob Orr campaign not too many years before. In my campaign, some time every day was spent on the phone trying to raise money. One of the amazing things about political fundraising is that the same people will give again and again.

The Wendy's Connection

In 1996, Goldsmith had a great advantage being mayor of our largest city with all the contractors, engineers, and other vendors just dying to contribute to the mayor's campaign for governor. I had several memorable fundraising events. Dave Thomas, the founder of Wendy's, flew his private jet to Indianapolis to have a fundraiser for me. I met him in Florida on a golf course. We were both advocates for adoptions. We became friends, and he spent all day at a golf outing fundraiser for me. He paid all his own expenses and gave me a personal check for $5,000.

The Sound Barrier Pilot Hangs In

Another friend who did yeoman service for me was General Chuck Yeager. We had fundraisers in Evansville, Indianapolis, and Fort Wayne, all in one day. He also spent the next day at fundraisers. Chuck Yeager is one of America's great heroes, and I am honored to have him as a friend. Having him speak at fundraisers on my behalf was a home run. My friend and campaign chairman, Dick Freeland, was also a great help in raising our money, as was my good buddy Darrell French and the French family. Nancy and Bob Irsay had a $1,000-per-couple fundraiser at their house. The good part was just about all the people they invited were Goldsmith contributors who didn't want to offend the Irsays.

Jug Eckert was also a tremendous help. The largest fundraiser we had was one at the Indianapolis Motor Speedway, hosted by Mari Hulman George and Jug. We had over 5,000 people, and we had it on the hottest day of the summer. We also did well with direct mail with contributions from regular folk all over the state. I was not real sorry I lost for myself, but I did feel bad about losing for all the people who busted their butts for me.

When the final count was in, Steve had about 290,000 votes, and I had about 204,000. If I had it to do all over again, I'd still have the same people running my campaign. They were great. They just needed a better candidate.

I would do several things different, but if "ifs and buts were candy and nuts, what a merry Christmas we would have." In the fall election, much to everybody's surprise, Frank O'Bannon beat Goldsmith by over 100,000 votes. In southern Indiana, where I had run the best, O'Bannon went through Goldsmith like cheese through a goat.

The Yard Sign Marshal

My daughter, Angie, all 110 pounds of her, got involved with my campaign. She is a graduate of Purdue, where she got a BS in nursing. She is a wonderful nurse who worked at Riley Hospital for 16 years. For the past two years, she has served as a helicopter nurse on LifeLine, where she helps save lives.

Unfortunately, Angie inherited several traits from me. The least injustice upsets her. She doesn't forget and forgive. She holds a grudge. She likes to argue, and I could go on and on. In fact, she might be worse than me, but I love her.

It seems someone was taking down my yard signs and replacing them with Goldsmith yard signs at intersections and right of ways. Angie appointed herself as the "yard sign marshal." On many nights, our big RV would roll out, and Angie and a couple of staffers would make the "get-even" runs. When my yard signs got torn down, they were left on the ground and replaced with a Goldsmith sign. Angie's MO was to take the Goldsmith sign with her while replacing it with a Vote for Early sign. She put the Goldsmith signs in the restroom of the RV, sometimes filling up the room. We might have lost the election, but thanks to Angie Schroeder, we won the yard sign contest hands-down.

I put my son Pat in an impossible "box." Steve Goldsmith had appointed Pat to the Capital Improvement Board, and Pat was elected as its chairman. It was a busy time, as they built both the baseball stadium (Victory Field) and Conseco Fieldhouse on Pat's watch. During the campaign, Pat had fundraisers for me, attended meetings, and did everything he could to help my campaign. To Steve Goldsmith's credit, he never leaned on Pat, and they worked together on the two major projects. Steve reappointed him to the board. My youngest son, Mike, was busy building houses, but he was also a "gung-ho" supporter of his dad.

The Credit Belongs (A Friend Sent This To Me)

The credit belongs to those who are actually in the arena, who strive valiantly; who know the great enthusiasms, the great devotions, and spend themselves in a worthy cause; who at the best, know the triumph of high achievement; and who, at the worst, if they fail, fail while daring greatly, so that their place shall never be with those cold and timid souls who know neither victory nor defeat.

Theodore Roosevelt

Chapter 18
Slating

Slating of candidates is a must in an urban area where the primary voters are just not familiar with the candidates. There are always goofs running. Some have been elected. (Actually, a lot of them have been elected!) Slating is a process where a committee or a group of party regulars interview all of the candidates who are running for a specific office. A slating fee, based on the pay scale of the job they are running for, is usually involved. It is usually 10 percent of the yearly pay for that particular office. I understand that Mayor Ballard had to pay a slating fee of $20,000. Usually, if a candidate is not slated, they get part or all of their money back, but not the slated candidate.

The Slating Committee then recommends one of the candidates for each office. This is really the party endorsement of the candidate, and this is who our Precinct Committeemen and volunteers will be working for in the primary election.

Dale Brown had a slating convention where every Precinct Committeemen and Vice voted on a voting machine to determine who was slated. Keith Bulen, on the other hand, usually had a small committee of 18–20 people, made up of finance people, Ward Chairman, and Precinct Committeemen. Keith appointed them, so they would generally do what Bulen wanted.

John Sweezy enlarged the process with each township and allotted so many slating spots. The Township Chairmen had the responsibility to fill those spots. There were usually as many as 50–60 people on the committee.

I figured out that if I asked my friends from other townships (usually Ward Chairmen or Vices) to tell their Township Chairman they wanted to serve on the slating committee, they were usually appointed. I liked that situation. I would get my friends on the slating committee, and generally they would vote for the county office holders: City Council members, judges, and sheriffs that I recommended. Back then, we were mostly electing Republicans, and most of our slated candidates won. This didn't always work, though. I was for Val Boring for judge, instead of Jim Payne.

Most of the time, former County Chairman John Sweezy didn't seem to want to get involved. For several years, most of the candidates I was for got slated and elected. Russ Brown and Jack Cottey (Township Chairmen of Lawrence and Warren townships) woke up and started doing the same thing. It upset my little deal, but good things don't last forever. After that, I had to negotiate with them on who was to get slated.

One of the Slating Committees that I remember most was one for the at-large candidate for the City Council. It was so heavy-handed, it was fun. The committee was made up of probably 65 members. My pals Bud Gohmann and Mike DeFabis were helping me get the votes for the candidates we wanted. There was an abundance of good candidates, but we had decided on the four we wanted. They were:

1. *Phil Borst:* My good friend Senator Larry Borst had called one and asked for my help. His son, Phil, was not known at the time, especially by anyone outside of Perry Township.

2. *Joyce Brinkman:* An incumbent and a party regular who would later have a distinguished career in the Legislature. She had made some of the people in Wayne Township mad, so she was at risk of not being slated.

3. *Paula Parker:* A new face who was the daughter of my good friend Buddy Parker.

4. *George Tintera:* An incumbent.

There were some other really good candidates, including Carlton Curry, who would later be on the City-County Council and is now a City of Lawrence Councilman, and Dan Evans, who is now the President of Clarion Health.

Dan Evans' speech somewhat did him in. During his speech he said, "I don't want to be obsequious." Of the 65 people on the committee, I would say one person knew what obsequious meant. That was Dottie Daniels, the Governor's mother. I was one who never heard of the word. Just a tip: If you are running for office, don't say you are or are not obsequious. It sounds like a disease or someone's sexual preference.

The rules stated that on the ballot you could vote for four, and we were to keep voting until someone had a majority of the 65 votes. We decided that we would "plunker vote": that is, only one vote per ballot. A plunker vote is when you only vote for one person when you have a choice to vote for several. We put Joyce Brinkman first, and the vote was 62 for Brinkman and 3 votes for others. On the second ballot, we took Borst. The vote was 62 for Borst and 3 for others.

After that vote, DeFabis came up to me, and said we have to stop doing this because it looks like it's wired. Well, Mike, it was. We had two more ballots with the same results. We thought that Paula Parker would be easiest to elect because of her father, so we saved her for last.

However, because the way we ran it, Paula had got zero votes on the first two ballots. Some of our African-American screeners were getting a little nervous because all they had was my word that we were going to help Paula.

The third ballot was taken, and Paula got the same 62 votes as did Tintera, the person who we picked on the fourth ballot.

Chapter 19
The Recount Commission

The 1984 Congressional race in the 8th District got nationwide attention. The race between Democrat Frank McCloskey and Republican Rick McIntyre ended in a virtual tie. Obviously, there was going to be a recount. Every county in the 8th District had their own recount. Democrat judges saw an issue one way, and Republican judges saw the same issues the other way. The rules for counting a ballot were different from county to county. Some counted hanging chads (where a punch card ballot still had the chad hanging on the ballot), and other counties didn't count them.

The recount numbers changed on a daily basis. Finally, Congress seated Frank McCloskey and said he won by four votes. The Democrat Congress, headed by Tip O'Neill, knew there were 20 unopened ballots in Evansville, Indiana that had come from service men. An Evansville newspaper researched the primary voting records of the people who had voted absentee and found that 16 of them or their households had voted Republican. When the Democrat Congress seated McCloskey, the Republicans walked out.

The Democrats had a 20-plus vote majority, and there was no reason to muscle one seat. There are those who opined that was the beginning of the rancor between the parties in Congress that continues today. I think that the reason Newt Gingrich took after Jim Wright was triggered by O'Neill's high-handed tactics. O'Neill's action was a prime example of "TAKING A BONE FROM A SKINNY DOG." You don't do that.

In 1995, the Legislature created a Recount Commission. This commission would do all the recounts for the state and federal offices. It was made up of three people that included the Secretary of State as chairman, and one person from each party appointed by their State Chairman.

In 1996, Evan Bayh was elected Secretary of State, and there were three recounts that fell to the newly created Recount Commission. Of the three recounts, two were legislative recounts. The other was the Congressional race from the South Bend area, where the Republican Congressman Jack Hiler won by about 70 votes.

As Secretary of State, Evan Bayh was the Chairman of the Commission; David Hamilton was the Democrat member, and I was the Republican member.

The Lipstick Ballot

One of the legislative races was in Richmond, Indiana where the Republican House Member (Janet Hibner) lost by one vote. Early on in that recount, we came upon a punch card ballot that had been folded in two and used by some lady to blot her lipstick. Immediately, Bayh and Hamilton declared it was a "marked ballot" and said it should not be counted (which would have made it a two-vote loss).

I made a speech that Abe Lincoln would have been proud of. I asked both Bayh and Hamilton their age, and I told them mine. Then I told them, with my infinite wisdom and experience that I had accumulated in my older age that anytime you got lipstick on anything, it was a mistake. They conferred and agreed. Unfortunately, the newspaper and TV picked up my lipstick theory.

The one-vote loss by Representative Hibner held up after our recounting the ballots. The other legislative race in the South Bend–Elkhart area was recounted, and the Republican won with very few recount problems.

The new recount law basically called for the State Board of Accounts to recount the ballots, and if there were any questions about a ballot, it was laid aside. The Recount Commission ruled on those ballots.

A Fair Bayh, a Republican Winner, and a Judge

The Congressional race to be recounted had originally shown Congressman Hiler winning by 70 votes. Basically, the recount was determining the voter's intent on the punch card ballots. Many of them did not have a clean punch next to the candidate's name, or the party in the case of a straight party vote. Some of the ballots were put in the machine upside down or backward. How do you unscramble that egg?

Congressman Hiler had another problem. One of the heavy-Republican precincts where Hiler had won by a large margin had a ballot security problem.

In that particular precinct, the inspector had not turned in his ballots and the count in that precinct.

The inspector's instructions had been to

1. Take all of his Election Day supplies to a certain point and deposit them in a semi-trailer.

2. Take the voted ballots, the unvoted ballots, and the paperwork showing the votes TO THE ELECTION BOARD, at the courthouse.

The inspector threw everything in the semi-trailer, including the ballots, and could not be reached or found that night. We had a ballot security issue. Could someone have tampered with those unguarded ballots? If those ballots were thrown out, Hiler would lose.

Because those ballots were not secured, the Hiler camp and I were concerned that they would be thrown out. As the recount progressed, I know that Evan Bayh was under a lot of pressure from his party people in that area to count Hiler out. I overheard one lady, a party official, tell Evan that he sure wasn't like his daddy. Evan stood fast. Examining every ballot that was laid aside by the State Board of Accounts was a large and laborious job.

Keep in mind we were mostly examining ballots that looked like the old IBM computer punch cards. The ballot fit in a device. The voter, using a stylus, would punch out the dot next to the name of the candidate that he or she wanted to vote for. We all three agreed if we saw a clear intent of the voter, this ballot should be counted.

Some of the ballots had the slightest dent in the paper ballot next to a name. I must admit I could see the Republican dents much clearer than the Democrat dents.

In the end, after several weeks, the ballots left out all night were counted. After examining in detail all of the questioned ballots, Congressman Hiler was declared the winner. I must admit I was very impressed with Evan Bayh, who I could tell from early on in the process wanted to be fair. Now he was also very likeable. (I just hated it when I decided I liked him.) Maybe it was because he was going to run for governor later. Whatever the reason, there was never a question in my mind that Evan Bayh and Dave Hamilton were not going to be party to counting out a Republican Congressman because of politics. Several years later, David Hamilton's name came up, seeking a federal judgeship where a Democrat was going to be picked. Without hesitation, I wrote a letter to Senator Lugar testifying to the character and honesty of David Hamilton and my hopes that he would support his appointment. Senator Lugar did that.

The One Trip in the New Used Car

Here is one little story. The Recount Commission decided that it was silly for all of us to drive every week. We usually stayed two or three days at a time. Evan decided to drive on one trip and came by my house to get me. He had a brand-new (to him) used car that he was very proud of. We stopped at a convenience store so I could get a cup of coffee and a pack of cigarettes. First, I spilled my coffee in his car, and then I smoked in his car. Evan looked like a person who had just drank a gallon of that stuff you take before you have a colonoscopy. Evan didn't volunteer driving after that.

Bipartisanship for Indiana Voters

When the recount was over, Evan, David, and I got together and helped draft legislation concerning recounts. All three of us were strong on "the clear intent of the voter." No one should be disfranchised over some technicality. The bill we helped draft passed and became law. Indiana would no longer be the laughing stock where we couldn't determine a winner in a Congressional race.

Chapter 20
The National Conventions

1968, Miami Beach: Nixon Nominated (Bad Hotel)

This was the year of the Chicago riots at the Democrat Convention. The Republican Convention followed the Democrats that year, and our security was unbelievable. The convention center was circled with a fence with razor wire, and federal troops were nearby.

I observed a Keith Bulen mummy-dummy deliver what looked like credentials to the front desk of our hotel. I heard him say, "Please give this envelope to Beurt SerVaas." Credentials were at a premium because this was a small convention center. I followed the mummy-dummy up and asked, "Did anybody leave something for Beurt SerVaas?" They handed me the credentials. Now I never said I was Beurt SerVaas, so my conscience is clear. Besides, it was just for the one night. Sorry, Beurt. My conscience has been hurting me for 40 years.

1972, Also Miami Beach: Nixon Nominated (Bad Hotel)

Watergate had surfaced but nobody thought much about it. Just another break-in. The Republican party chartered a real-big, stretch DC8 to haul our people down there and back. After the convention, we were ready to come back home. The plane took off, and having flown out of the Miami airport before, I thought it strange when we came back around and circled the airport at a low altitude. Now the Who's Who of the Republican party was on that plane. Doc Bowen and Bob Orr were both aboard, and they had just been nominated as governor and Lt. Governor.

It seems the reason for our fly-over was because our landing gear was locked at about a 45-degree angle. It wouldn't go down, and it wouldn't go up. The reason for the pass-by was so the people in the tower could look. The captain announced the predicament, and there was a lot of concern. One of our Marion County attorneys lost it, and Dr. Denny Nichols, an MD and the county coroner, had to give him a shot to knock him out because he was so upset.

I was sitting right behind Seth Denbo and one of his friends. They were praying out loud as the time went by. I was not sure I wanted to call to God's attention that Seth was even on the plane. A two-hour trip turned into a four-hour trip. At one point, we dumped fuel for a foam landing. Finally, they thought they had it fixed, but fire trucks and ambulances followed us down the runway. It was obviously fixed. I'm here, ain't I?

1976, Kansas City: Ford versus Reagan

Our hotel was probably 30 or 40 miles from the convention center. Later on, I will explain the Jenner-Rockefeller episode and how the vote was for a "resolution," not using the Ford and Reagan names. Bill Ruckelshaus, from Indianapolis, was prominently touted as one of those who Ford was considering for Vice President because Rockefeller was not going to run again for V.P. Bill had run for Congress in the 1964 primary and was beaten by Don Tabbert. He had later been the Speaker of the House and was Nixon's first Environmental Protection Agency director. He had also been head of the FBI and was Attorney General for a short time during the time Nixon was about to resign.

Because we were 30 or 40 miles from our hotel, we had a rather lengthy bus ride from our hotel to the convention center.

One evening, we were going to the convention, and our route was through a rather poor section of Kansas City. It was summer time, and there were lots of people on the streets. Realizing we were probably going to the convention, and were thus Republicans, the people on the street were yelling some uncomplimentary things about us and our party while our bus crawled through their neighborhoods. It really wasn't bothering anybody, but the Reverend Mayor Bill Hudnut was near one of the open windows. He yelled back, in a very loud voice, "Poverty sucks!" Now Bill was just elected and was a new guy on the block. Most on the bus knew he was a preacher. You could have heard a mouse get an erection, it got so quiet on our bus. I guess some of the people on the bus from out in the state probably thought this was a strange response from a minister.

1980, Detroit: Reagan Nominated (Good Hotel)

Keith Bulen was one of the people who Reagan had put in charge of running the convention. Keith had gone to Detroit early with his whole tribe of mummy-dummys. Bill Colbert, Bud Gohmann, Jim Cummins, Nick Longworth…

the list goes on. Keith had it organized to a T. This was an exciting convention for me. I loved Reagan. He and Nancy and he had been to our home, and I was his state campaign director.

The other exciting thing was that Senator Lugar had a great chance to be nominated for Vice President. We were told authoritatively that it was between Lugar and George Bush. (I still have some Reagan/Lugar buttons we had made up.) Senator Howard Baker, from Tennessee, was pushing for Lugar and was one of Reagan's insiders. At one point during the convention, Baker had come down to our delegation to tell Lugar it looked good.

Every convention I've been to had a telephone at the chair of that state's convention chairman. At Detroit, we had two phones. One was red, and the red one was supposed to be wired into the Reagan brain trust. After three or four sessions, the red phone rang. I was sitting a couple rows back, next to Lugar. The call was for me. I jumped up and literally climbed over people to get to the Red Phone. I was sure it was Bulen, calling to tell me to tell Lugar that he was the choice. Was I excited! Breathlessly, I said hello. The voice on the other end asked whether this was Rex Early. I said yes. Then the voice said, "I want to order two pizzas, one with sausage, and one with plain cheese. And hold the anchovies." It was Tom Keating, The Indianapolis Star's great reporter and writer. He had somehow talked someone with Red Phone access to call me. I'm sure he got a kick watching me stepping on my fellow delegates to get to the phone.

One evening after a session, several of us decided to go to dinner in downtown Detroit. We had heard of a very good Italian restaurant close to the convention. We asked a policeman (there was a lot of security around the convention.) about how far away was the restaurant. He told us it was about five blocks from where we were. I asked "How long will it take us to get there if we walked?" He replied, "I don't know, nobody has ever made it." Detroit is a tough town.

1984, Dallas: Reagan's Second Term (Bad Hotel)

We all loved Reagan, as did the rest of the country. He had appointed me to the American Battle Monuments Commission, something I was very proud of. One of the videos shown at the convention was President Reagan's great speech to the Rangers at Pointe du Hoc at Normandy Beach. I was just a few yards away from him when he gave that speech.

1988, New Orleans: George H. W. Bush and Dan Quayle (Worst Hotel Ever)

Our hotel was at the end of the runway at the New Orleans airport. The hotel and the restaurant were reportedly closed right after the convention. I think they had Board of Health problems. We were light years away from the French Quarter and a long way from the convention center. We were there at the convention when George H. W. Bush said, "Read my lips. No new taxes!" Later on, he wished he had never said that.

The exciting thing was the nomination of our own, Dan Quayle, to be the Vice President. The Sunday before the Wednesday that Dan was named as Bush's choice for V.P., we were at a party in the backyard of our convention host.

Our host was a Republican state senator. I was talking to Dan about his name having been floated, and I can tell you that he didn't have a clue he was being picked. He knew his name had been floated by the news people as being considered, but that Sunday, he thought it was just a joke.

Later in the week, our Senator, Dan, scheduled a party that he was hosting for us at the hotel. It was to start at 2 p.m. When Dan didn't show up, and he was the host, we wondered why. It grew later and later, and then we got the word. Bush had picked Dan Quayle as his running mate. How exciting for the Indiana delegation! Dan did come back for the party, but by then, he was surrounded by Secret Service people and presidential campaign staffers. At the convention that night, the national press besieged the Indiana delegates. The national press wanted to talk to anyone who knew Dan or anything about him. I was probably interviewed ten times, as were the rest of the delegation. They were already hostile because they hadn't been given a heads-up, and they had very little background on him. I think that hostility followed Dan the first few months of the campaign. It wasn't his fault.

The Bush team could have handled the whole announcement of Dan being chosen a lot differently.

1992, Houston: George H. W. Bush's Second (The very best hotel in Houston. We had the Vice President with us.)

As a member of the National Committee, I had to go to Houston a week early to attend various meetings. I was also elected as chairman of the Indiana delegation, which meant

I got to announce our state's vote. You have heard them before:

> The great State of Indiana, the State of Lincoln's
>   boyhood,
> the home of our great Senators Dick Lugar
>   and Dan Coats,
> and Skinny Alexander and Seth Denbo,
> and also the home of Decker melons and on and on,
> casts 54 votes for George Bush.

Boy, I was in tall cotton.

Linley Pearson's staff suggested that I let Linley give the count. I told them that if I died between their request and the time for the vote, it was okay for Linley to make the announcement. However, if I was alive, thank you very much, I will give the count.

Before the convention, Rich Bond, our national chair, asked me for a breakdown of the delegates I was going to have. He was looking for diversity. I told him I was sending 54 white males. He almost had a stroke. We made a deal. He would give me two floor passes for every woman or minority that I sent as a delegate. I was just joking with him when I told him all white males, and we ended up with 30 or 40 floor passes. With that many floor passes, I got all of our alternates and guests plenty of floor time.

Ray Geist, the Decatur County Chairman, was in charge of the floor passes, and he made sure all the Indiana guests got to get on the floor. I made a deal with our delegates that they let their alternates share time. Because it was Dan Quayle's home state, I was assigned to make several motions from the floor, and I also got to make the motion to elect Vice President Quayle by acclamation.

Being part of the program with some motions I was supposed to make, I lost a chance to fly with President Bush on Air Force One to Indianapolis, where he was speaking to either a VFW convention or an American Legion convention. Ron Kaufman, one of President Bush's aides, set it up for me and put me on the manifest, but I had a part on the program for that afternoon's session and had to cancel out on the plane flight. A lot of my pals, like Jug Eckert, who helped me get the party out of debt, ended up as delegates.

Jug took over the hotel bar the first night. Nobody from Indiana could pay for a drink except Jug for the entire convention. I had also asked many of our major Indiana corporations if they wouldn't like to throw a party for our delegations while in Houston. After all, besides the V.P. being there, our senators and congressmen plus a Who's Who of Indiana was going to be there. We had three or four out-of-sight parties and luncheons, courtesy of our Indiana hosts. The best luncheon was hosted by Jerry and Edna Mann.

On one of the first nights, our Houston host family threw a party for the Indiana delegation at their home. He was a big-time oil man, and his host party was very memorable.

I had gotten to know Ken Bode, who had been the NBC political person. In 1992, he signed on with CNN as their political consultant at the two conventions.

One night, Bode had sent Gene Randall, the CNN reporter on the floor, to interview me on national TV. Randall asked me whether it made a difference on how we were treated, seeing as how we had the Vice President from our state. I told him that first of all, we had the best seats in the convention hall, but more importantly, I had been coming to these events since 1968, and it was the first time we had a hotel that they didn't rent the rooms by the hour. They immediately switched to their campaign center where Bernard Shaw was laughing his butt off. I guess he found my answer funny. I also got to spend 30 minutes on C-SPAN, answering call in questions on national TV. Hillbillies can get on TV and answer questions, too.

After the convention, I rode on Air Force Two, at Dan Quayle's invitation, to Gulfport, Mississippi, where both President Bush and Quayle attended a rally. We then flew to Washington, DC, where I stayed the night. I got picked up the next morning and accompanied the Vice President on Air Force Two to Fort Wayne. The whole convention was a great experience, and I got to share a lot of it with my Indianapolis pals who helped me get rid of our debt.

Every dog has his day, and the 1992 convention was mine.

1996, San Diego: Bob Dole Nominated (Back to a Fair Hotel)

I was the Indiana Chairman for Dole-Kemp, and as such, had to go to several meetings. The convention was sort of lackluster after Houston. Also, there was a feeling that was sort of prevalent that we were not going to win. Indiana was one of the few Midwestern states to carry Dole.

While out there, I visited the Marine Corps base at Camp Pendleton. That base, among other things, was the staging base for the Marine Corps where everyone going overseas assembled until they shipped out. It had all changed, and I couldn't find our "tent city" where we waited and trained until we got on the USS Montrose to go overseas.

2000, Philadelphia: George W. Bush Nominated (Good Hotel)

It was a good convention. Victory was in the air. Bush was great. I am just spoiled after the '92 convention.

There is a country-western song about someone rather being in hell than in New York City. I don't go to New York City.

Chapter 21
Stupid Republican Moves

I've seen some crazy things in politics, but at least two of them involved the Indiana State Chamber of Commerce. One was when the Chamber of Commerce decided that Indiana's prevailing wage law should be changed or abolished. Two was when they decided to beat Jerry Bales in District 60.

The First Stupid Move

President Ronald Reagan had captured the "working man" vote. This included many of our friends who belonged to a union. Especially the building trades. The economy was good. Folks bought a nice house. They had two cars and a fishing boat. They were pro-family, pro-gun, pro-life, and they liked Reagan's rock-hard stand against Communism. They were not wild about the Democrats' stand on gay marriage and some of the social issues. Many of them were voting Republicans until we decided to hit them right in the face with the prevailing wage issue.

They stormed the State House with people. The bill the Republicans passed did nothing that was provable as far as lowering the cost of school and other governmental buildings. It was all B.S. We, the Republicans, lost the next election as far as the legislature was concerned, and we have never gotten them back. You don't monkey with people's livelihood.

The Second Stupid Move

The second stupid thing was when the Republican State Chairman and the Chamber of Commerce decided to beat Representative Jerry Bales, of District 60 from Bloomington, in the primary. Sure enough, they beat him in a primary election with someone who could never be elected, but the Chamber of Commerce liked him. Peggy Welch, a Democrat, was elected and will probably be re-elected as long as she wants to run. Jerry Bales was the only Republican who could ever have won that district, and just think since 1998 how many times one more vote would have made a difference.

And One More Thing

I also thought it was a little disingenuous for the Chamber of Commerce people to be on Greg Garrison's WIBC talk-radio program bemoaning the home owners' property tax problem we have in Marion County, when the Chamber of Commerce and the Indiana Manufacturers Association did everything they could to get the "fair-market value" method of assessing property made into law. They surely knew that residential property taxes would go up dramatically while business taxes would go down.

Chapter 22
The Erosion of Political Parties

I lived and loved politics. It's competition even after you get too old to play sports. However, the two-party system has eroded. Some of the erosion was caused by the courts. Other erosion was caused by people. Part of my party's erosion has been caused by office holders we have elected but who have no bedrock principles. When it comes to party principles versus special interests, guess who wins?

Erosion Number One:
Reapportioning Legislative Districts

The weakening of the parties started in the mid-1960s, when several state and federal lawsuits concerning reapportioning of their state legislature and Congressional districts were filed.

There were some inequities. For instance, Andy Jacobs was in Congress, and he represented 790,000-plus people. At the same time, Lee Hamilton represented 290,000-plus people. In Indiana, Nelson Grills (a Democrat lawyer who served in the senate) won a lawsuit in a Marion County Court with a Democrat judge. The court declared our state legislative maps as unconstitutional. The state legislators ignored that ruling until 1972 when they drew a new map with three member Legislative Districts. Prior to that, all of our 11 house candidates ran on a county-wide basis. When all 11 house members were running at-large, the Republican organization could nominate or drop an incumbent with ease. It was much more difficult to beat an incumbent in a small district than it was on a county wide district.

When I was slated and nominated to the Legislature in 1962, Dale Brown (our County Chairman) dumped an incumbent legislator in favor of me.

The first districts, drawn by the Republicans, were three-member districts. The gerrymandered districts were drawn to concentrate the strong Democrat neighborhoods into one district. 1972 was a good Republican year, and on a county-wide basis, we would have won all the seats. One district selected three African-American Democrats: "Skinny" Alexander, Julia Carson, and Bill Crawford. All the voting machines listed the candidates alphabetically in the primary. (It sure helped if your name began with A, B, or C.)

The Republican Party could live with a three-member district. It was big enough geographically, the candidates were generally unknown to most of the electorate, and they were beholden to the "party" to be nominated and elected.

Soon after that, again with federal and state pressure, the next maps were forced to go to single-member districts. A legislator could build his own fiefdom and stay there forever if he didn't screw up too bad. The maps were drawn to overload some of the districts, so whether Democrat or Republican, you could never have a competitive race. After all, the legislators in power were drawing the maps, and they were going to design lose-proof districts for themselves, if possible—and they did.

The single member district maps was a signal that campaign contributions from special-interest groups could go right to the candidate and not the political organization. IT WAS A DARK DAY FOR THE POLITICAL PARTIES. The new maps led to legislators holding office forever.

Both Senator Larry Borst and Senator Bob Garton were approaching 40 years in the Legislature. Because most the legislators' constituents have no idea how he or she votes, it is almost impossible to beat them. They both represented strong Republican districts, and there was NO way they would ever lose to a Democrat challenger.

Both got defeated in a primary election on basically one issue: A healthcare package for part-time legislators had passed without any publicity. The plan was so inclusive and would have been so expensive to buy that Donald Trump couldn't have afforded it. The lifetime package not only covered the legislators but wives, ex-wives, and probably family pets. At a time when many citizens were struggling to pay for their healthcare coverage, passing that healthcare package for life for legislators was a monumental mistake on the legislators' part.

When our founding fathers brought forth a representative republic, I am sure that they never envisioned people staying for 40 years. They should remember rule # 18. The cemeteries are full of "indispensable" people.

Former Senator Larry Borst now works for one of the big law firms. They probably needed an in-house veterinarian.

Erosion Number Two:
Direct Primaries

In 1968, Doc Bowen was beaten by Ed Whitcomb for governor at the State Convention. Thanks to Keith Bulen, Seth Denbo (the 8th District Chair), Orvis Beers from Fort Wayne, Ted Sendak from Lake County, and Buena Chaney from Vigo County, Doc never had a chance.

Four years later (in 1972), Doc was the people's choice, and he figured the convention would be a walk-over. Wrong! Keith Bulen had been the National Committeeman for two years and desperately wanted another term. The vote for National Committeeman is always the day before the convention. Even though it was obvious that Bowen would win, Keith cut a deal with outgoing Whitcomb's forces, who controlled the state party. Keith would be elected National Committeeman, and he (and Marion County) would support Bill Sharp, who was running for governor against Doc.

Keith kept his word, and the large majority of the Marion County delegates (around 200 delegates) voted for Sharp even though they felt it was for naught. Bowen was once again furious. He had never liked Bulen.

Doc, upon being elected governor, pushed legislation that put the governor, senators, and Lt. Governor on the primary ballot. The Lt. Governor was taken off the primary ballot and back on this convention in later years. IN MY OPINION, THIS WAS A MAJOR MISTAKE. No longer did the party faithfully pick its top candidates, no longer could a would-be candidate for governor or senator travel the state in search of delegates' votes. The real grass-roots leaders of the parties are ignored. Probably the worst consequence of getting rid of the convention is the cost of intra-party primary fights.

The last knockdown drag-out was 1996. The candidates spent 12 million dollars in the primary. That was the year I ran and raised about 3 million, and got out-spent by Goldsmith, who spent around 7.5 million. Pat Rooney, Bob Garton, and George Witwer spent around 2 million. Most all of that money could have been spent in the fall if we had conventions.

Also, who in the world can run for governor if they have limited resources and do not live in one of the "populated counties" where campaign money can be raised? I firmly believe that whoever can spend the most will win. Unfortunately, name ID is everything in a primary.

We have people in both parties, God bless them, who will vote in a primary regardless of what they know about the candidates. It is their God-given constitutional right to vote in their party's primary, regardless of what they know about the candidates. If they recognize a name, that is who they will vote for. I truly believe that Lee Harvey Oswald would get votes. It's a name they remember from somewhere.

You get name ID on a state-wide basis, by buying it on the radio and especially on TV. Who furnishes the money for buying TV? Well, it isn't the Little Sisters of the Poor. It is special-interest groups.

The Indianapolis Star was a big proponent of the candidate being chosen in the primaries, and not the convention. They thought that would be the more "honest" way of picking our governors and senators. WRONG.

Dick Lugar ran for Senate and was nominated in two

conventions. Bill Jenner was nominated in a convention, and so were Matt Welsh, Roger Branigan, Harold Handley, Birch Bayh, and many other great Hoosiers who served their state.

A Big Mistake.

Erosion Number Three:
Greed and the "County Chairman for Life"

Indiana license branches were given out as patronage. The Republican Chairman, the governor's office, and the Department of Motor Vehicles (DMV) decided how many branches each county needed, and the County Chairman would either manage the branches or appoint a manager.

The branches were run like a for-profit business, which was exactly what they were.

In the smaller counties, the license branches were usually manned by patronage workers, precinct committeemen and -women, and maybe a relative or two of the County Chairman. The profits over and above the salaries were given to the party to operate on. The system worked although it did disturb the "out party" where they had to pay a fee that went to this governor's party.

As I said before, in the smaller counties, the license branches threw off enough for some jobs and party expenses. In the larger counties, it was a BONANZA. The Marion County branches were set up as a private corporation, and the amount that went to the party was negligible because of the election laws governing how much a corporation could contribute to the party.

Is it any wonder that some of the County Chairmen did not want to lose this gold mine? They changed the party rules to make it virtually impossible to beat a County Chairman, especially in the urban areas. It truly guaranteed the COUNTY CHAIRMAN FOR LIFE. It was rumored that the Marion County License Branch Corporation generated around $400,000 per year to the corporation's principals.

They did this by changing the term of office from two years to four years for Committeemen and County Chairman. Also, the party's County Convention was changed to where the elected precinct Committeemen only had an opportunity to vote for county chairman on his or her third year in office. Many of the elected committeemen had either moved or resigned prior to the third year, and of course, they were replaced by the County Chairman's appointed precinct Committeeman, many of whom didn't have to live in the precinct. He only had to be a friend of the Chairman. In today's world, in the larger counties, probably 85 percent of the Committeemen are appointed. They don't try to find Committeemen to run; they just appoint. There is no doubt some of the appointed Committeemen take their job seriously and try to perform. But many others are there only to vote for the County Chairman's continued tenure.

Right now, one of the larger Indiana Counties (Allen County) has Republican loyalists who want a new County Chairman. The Chairman is there for life if he wants to be because he appointed many of the precinct Committeemen.

The license branches were taken away from the parties and given back to the state in 1988. Nevertheless, the "County Chairman for Life" system still exists.

When the Marion County Republicans wanted to change the County Chairman in 1999, they had to make certain commitments and monetary considerations to get the sitting Chairman to step down.

Erosion Number Four:
The Law Firms

The party's power has declined while the large law firms have become more powerful and influential.

When Governor Mitch Daniels was first deciding whether to run for governor, we had a meeting. During that meeting, Mitch made mention of how the big law firms have an inordinate amount of influence with both the state and city government. I agreed with him.

That is still true today; maybe more so.

When the election results showed that Greg Ballard would be next mayor of Indianapolis, one of the big law firms was on him like a duck after a June bug. It seems that they controlled the transition. In fact, it was almost comical, watching the other law firms scrambling to get a seat at the mayor's table. It was a GRAND day in Indianapolis when Ballard won.

I think Greg Ballard could be a great mayor. He has the personality and all the tools. Certainly, being a Lt. Colonel in the Marine Corps proves that he has the ability to lead. I hope he remembers that people were voting for him and not a law firm.

Speaking of Greg Ballard, it looks to me that one of Democrat Mayor Peterson's largest contributors (if not his largest contributor) came from an engineering firm. Ballard's new Chief of Staff was the Indianapolis manager of that engineering firm. I bet the other engineering firms are saying, "Heads, they win; tails, I lose!"

Large law firms dominate the political process

Now the large firms have always had lawyers deeply

involved with the political process. When I was in the legislature, Kurt Pantzer, Sr. (the senior partner in what is now Barnes and Thornburg) had a breakfast meeting every Monday morning for the Marion County delegation. I mentioned before that Joe Daniels, the senior partner of Baker and Daniels, had at one time been the Republican District Chairman. When the Ku Klux Klan had an inordinate amount of influence in the state Republican Party, their lawyer had been a political powerhouse. In fact, one of our Republican mayors of Indianapolis was impeached because of his relationship with the Klan.

Since the decline in influence and power of the political party, the large law firms have stepped into the void and have become more and more influential and powerful.

Some of their influence and power is just perception. If the Chief of Staff is a partner or picked by a law firm, you might assume that his or her law firm might have some influence.

When I first got into politics, the power and influence was vested in the party. This was because the governor, Lt. Governor, and the senatorial candidates, as well as the Appellate Court and the Supreme Court judges, were nominated by a party convention.

With the Marion County screening process being directed by the politicians and the County Chairman, the city and county office holders and legislators were also beholden to the party.

The other state offices, Attorney General, Lt. Governor, Secretary of State, Auditor, Treasurer, and Superintendant of Public Instruction are all still picked by the party convention. Unfortunately, without the governor being picked by the delegates, there is a noticeable lack of interest by what used to be the grass-roots.

The Lt. Governor candidate will always be picked by the nominated governor, and the special-interest groups will work the delegations hard to get their candidate in the other offices.

The law firms will always be interested in the auditor and treasurer offices, and especially the state bond bank because of the lucrative bond business. Legal fees must be made from the Secretary of State office because I have noticed the law firms are also interested there. The Attorney General's office also hires "outside counsel," but it usually goes to some of the small firms.

As far as the Superintendent of Public Instruction, the law firms probably wouldn't care if they nominated Lee Harvey Oswald.

The neat thing about law firms' politics is they are all Mickey Mantles. (They can hit from the right or the left side.) They have political influence with both the Democrats and the Republicans. They can switch-hit faster than a cat can scratch its butt. Except for the inconvenience, they probably don't care whether the Republicans or the Democrats win.

It's, "Heads, they win; tails, they win, too!"

Campaigns are Candidate Oriented

What has changed since the Brown and Bulen days is that political campaigns are NOW TOTALLY CANDIDATE ORIENTED. Every candidate running for election or re-election raises and spends money for THEIR campaigns. It used to be that the PARTIES raised and spent most of the money. In today's world, most of the yard signs or TV and radio ads don't even mention whether the candidate is a Republican or Democrat. The most-effective advertising is a 30-second TV ad. In the Marion County media market, one week's worth of TV ads, which would have 1,100 rating points, costs well more than $100,000 dollars. The Chicago market, which serves all of northwest Indiana, is probably double or triple that rate. You also have to consider TV advertising in Evansville, Terre Haute, Fort Wayne, Cincinnati, Louisville, and South Bend.

Now where in the world is a candidate going to get that kind of money? WELL, IT DON'T COME FROM THE LITTLE SISTERS OF THE POOR.

A lot of big money comes from the special-interest groups. The law firms represent them. I do know that there is still a group of hard-core Republicans who will donate because they believe in the candidate and their party. When I was State Chairman, I was always amazed that direct mail would raise money. Many contributed but $10 or $20, but they were "believers."

There is no statutory limit on what the individual attorneys can donate. Of course, there is a limit what a corporation can donate.

The Basket Carriers

In my church every Sunday, a man walks down the rows of pews and passes a basket. I always put money in it. I watch him, and he dumps his basket into a bigger basket. Now the guy with the big basket goes down and lays it on the altar. The priest gives him a blessing and probably calls him by name, even though I might have put more money in the basket than he did. But he's the basket carrier. He gets the credit. I try to shy away from basket carriers even though I must admit I've been one.

Law firms have great basket carriers

Some of the law firms have great "basket carriers."

One of my acquaintances, who is a lawyer, is the Indiana champion basket carrier. We had a fundraiser for George W. Bush in 1999. I think I raised about $59,000. I also maxed out as an individual at $2,000. My acquaintance, the Indiana champion basket carrier, gave the same amount that I did. However, he was on the stage, and I was at the back table. He took my $59,000 and other people's contributions and "carried the basket" to George W. They call that "bundling."

I understand he gets invited to the White House, and I'm not even on the Christmas card list. I was born at night, but not last night, and I got a "bundle" number from the Fred Thompson campaign. All I want is back on the Christmas card list.

Now that Fred Thompson is no longer a candidate for President, it looks like I've got four more years without a Christmas card from the White House.

Besides being expert basket carriers, law firms have people available for campaigns. They are usually sharp people. By virtue of their jobs and their firms, some of them are able to work full time on campaigns strictly as a volunteer. In one of our last governor's campaigns, one of the law firms was able to send a whole cadre of young, bright lawyers, most of whom ended up with a job in the administration. Some even helped appoint some of the boards and commissions. How strong is that, if you go back to the firm and practice law? You don't think they would be well-received if they appear before the boards that they helped appoint?

Influence is the name of the game.

Several years ago, if someone had a problem with some branch of government, you would get in touch with one of the party leaders, and maybe he could unscramble the egg for you. Forget that now. Get the right attorney out of the right firm.

Besides representing clients, law firms want to be hired by the government. Unbeknownst to the average tax payer, government and governmental units spend millions of dollars on legal fees.

These are taxing units of government that the boards have been appointed by elected officials. In addition to the taxing units hiring attorneys, many of the government departments hire attorneys.

I am sure that there are occasions when legal questions come up, and good legal counsel is needed. I do think there ought to be some oversight on their budgets for legal services.

I had a friend appointed to a quasi-governmental board. Every board meeting, one or two attorneys showed up, each costing $300 per hour just to sit in a board meeting, and they were seldom called upon.

The big banana is legal counsel for the endless amount of bond transaction government has. The city's pension bond is coming up soon. It will be interesting (with all our property tax problems) whether this 500 million–dollar bond issue will still have a one-percent fee going to its attorney. Folks, that's 5 million dollars. I'd like to see the time sheet on that one.

I have heard stories about legal fees where the legal bills would support the military budget on some of the small Latin American countries.

Is My Side My Attorney's Side?

Another thing that does boggle my mind is how one law firm can represent clients who have 180 degrees difference on the same issue. They do it. I'm not a lawyer, so I thought it might be a conflict, but I've been told that they can do that because they have a "Chinese Wall" between them. I don't know what a Chinese Wall is. I was stationed in Japan, and they didn't have Japanese walls. It would be a little disheartening to hire an attorney to pursue an issue only to find out that attorneys on the other side are in the same firm. What if they are paying their lawyer more than I'm paying mine? I thought there was some commission who looked at things like that, but I've been told they only go after attorneys who have drinking problems or don't show up at court. That shows you how much I know. I do understand that Baker and Daniels stays away from those multi-client situations.

There will always be politics in government.

1. Party politics (whose power and influence is declining.)
2. Personal politics, where you do business with people you know, not necessarily with just Republicans or Democrats.
3. Law firms' politics are sort of a hybrid. Like Mickey Mantle, they can hit from both sides, and they are very effective as far as influence is concerned.

Now nobody wants to talk about SELLING INFLU-ENCE. But I did read a recent newspaper article that surprised me. The article was in the Indianapolis Business Journal dated November 19, 2007. A gentleman, Bob Birge, President of Law Firm Marketing Network, said: "Political influence within a law firm is very important." In talking about the Republican County Chairman's law firm, he said: "Now, at least for the next four years, they (the Chairman's law firm) are positioned pretty well to do any regulatory or governmental type of work."

When L. Keith Bulen was Republican County Chairman, his law partner was Charley Castor. Now Charley Castor was a very good lawyer. Castor registered to lobby, and The Indianapolis Star went berserk. It was front-page material about selling influence, and Castor immediately changed his mind and withdrew as a lobbyist. The Star's Eugene Pulliam and Bob Early would have a coronary arrest at how things are done today.

It seems to me there are four divisions in the big firms.

1. The Influence Pedaling Division: They will represent you with governmental agency if you have something to sell or lease to them: things such as lottery computers or engineering services, or practically anything that government buys. Also, representing clients in the regulated industries and firms that just moved into the state and want lawyers with influence.

2. The Influence Lawyering Division: They seek employment of their firm to represent any governmental units. The bonding area is one of the real lucrative

areas, but they will represent any unit of government, school boards, and quasi-governmental units. Any unit of government that has its own "taxing" authority is fair game.

3. Lobbying Division: The law firms do not dominate lobbying although they all have people in the firm who are good. They are just not always the best. Lobbyists who have personal relationship with the legislators are the most effective. I am sure that in the future, they will be listed in the Yellow Pages under "Influence."

4. Lawyering Division: They just practice law like they used to.

I've been told that, "Beauty is a light switch away." Just remember: Governmental help is just a telephone call away if you call the right law firm.

I am not concerned with the law firms' activities. That is certainly fair game and taxpayers' dollars are not paying the fees. We should be concerned with the legal fees that are paid by the government using taxpayers' money. Where are the old Indianapolis Star people—Bob Early, Bo Conner, Dick Cady, and Kathleen Johnson—when you need them?

I do wonder sometimes whether the great legal minds like Joe Daniels, Kurt Pantzer, John Alexander, and Jim Donato (all of whom I knew) would think of the shift from the practice of law to "Governmental Services," or whatever they might call it.

Just something I think about when I don't have anything else to do.

Chapter 23
Ed Lewis, Evan Bayh,
and John Mutz

Ed Lewis was a dandy. He was very protective and loyal to his friends. He had a big heart, and you were a lucky man to be a friend of Ed Lewis.

Ed and I had lunch once per week, always at the same restaurant. He was under strict orders by his doctor not to smoke or drink. These lunches were long, and Ed smoked and drank a few Bloody Marys. He would laugh about "cheating" a little.

I had met Ed probably around 1984, when he called me and asked whether I would meet him for lunch. When I got there, Larry Conrad was also there.

It seemed that my old friend and Ed's old friend, Noble Pearcy, was on hard times, and Ed wanted to help him. Noble had been the Marion County Prosecutor in the '60s and '70s. He had gotten into a shit-fight with The Indianapolis Star about how he handled some investigation. The fight got so bad that Nobe and his buddy, Bob Fields (who was sheriff) had two of The Star's reporters arrested and put in jail. (A bad decision on Nobe's part.) Needless to say, the next time that Noble had to run for re-election, he did not have the endorsement from The Star.

Lewis, Conrad, and Early Help an Old Friend

I had heard that Nobe had some health problems, but I had no idea how bad they were. If you could have something wrong with you, Nobe had it. Ed found out that in addition to Nobe's health problems, he had some serious financial problems. Nobe had taken out a bank loan for around $25,000, which was way past due, and the bank was pressing. He also had some other debts. Besides a meager pension and Social Security, he and his wife's only income was his wife's (Hazel's) job at a school cafeteria. Nobe knew he was not long for this world, and he was beside himself wondering how he and his wife were going to pay the bank loan. Ed suggested that he and Conrad work the Democrats and that I work the Republicans to raise the money to pay off Nobe's loan. We raised the money in a couple of weeks and gave it to Nobe's wife, who paid off the bank.

Bud Gohmann, the Marion County Clerk, also helped as he gave Hazel, Nobe's wife, a job in the clerk's office. We asked that Nobe not know that we did this because he would have been embarrassed. After helping Nobe Pearcy, Ed and I became friends. We both liked to bet the ponies and gamble a little. Ed and my wife even owned a horse together. His name was Lash, and he wasn't much. When Ed and I went to the track, we always bet on our own horses, even when we knew they couldn't win. It was a "pride" thing. Hope springs eternal when you own a horse.

Goodbye, Engineering; Hello, Insurance

I sold my business, Mid-States Engineering, in 1982, and I was getting bored watching reruns of The Little Rascals and The Three Stooges. Ed suggested we go into the insurance business (something neither one of us knew much about). I went to an "insurance school." I took and passed the state test, and got my state insurance license.

I shopped around and found a young man who had majored in insurance in college and was working as an underwriter with CNA (a large insurance company). He knew a lot about insurance, and I hired him to run our new agency. Twenty-four years later, he's still running it. I named the agency Carlisle Insurance Agency, doing business as Consolidated Insurance Services. We were struggling for a couple of years, but finally we turned the corner and started to make some money. I bought Ed Lewis out. I think Ed just wanted to find me something to do, besides watch The Little Rascals, and he sure didn't want to sell insurance.

The Governor's Race: Where Does He Live?

In 1987, Ed and I were busy. I was raising money for John Mutz for governor, and Ed was raising money for Evan Bayh for governor. In a close race, Bayh beat John Mutz. John Mutz is one smart guy who understands politics. He would have made a great governor. John had been involved in Marion County politics. He had to. His mother-in-law was Marcia Hawthorne. She had been a Republican legislator and had also held a county office. She was known far and wide for expressing her opinion (on everything).

The Mutz campaign was headed up by Mike McDaniel.

We did a lot of direct mail, and our direct mail guy was a young Republican from Texas named Karl Rove. I wonder what ever happened to him?

The Mutz campaign made one monumental mistake, which I think cost us the election. Evan Bayh had grown up and was raised in Washington, DC. His father, of course, was Birch Bayh, Indiana's senior senator and a former Indiana legislator from the Terre Haute area. Evan had gone to college at Indiana University. We raised the question of his residency. Of course, the governor of Indiana had to be a resident of Indiana. The attorney for the Mutz team was from one of the big law firms. He was absolutely convinced we could win a lawsuit contesting Evan's residency. He had researched the whole question, and we would win.

The Mutz committee met, and we discussed the whole residency question. There were some who thought that the lawsuit should be filed, but others were opposed to it. I was against it. The vote was to go ahead and challenge the residency. We were ready to file our complaint with the court. Our attorney, who was sure we could win, informed us he could not represent us in court because his partners didn't want him to. We should have backed off then. We filed the complaint. The judge ruled, basically, that your residence is where you say it is. One thing I know about Hoosiers: THEY ARE STRONG ON FAIR. I am sure that lots of Hoosiers thought that getting Evan out of the race on something they thought was a technicality was NOT FAIR. We should have said, "We don't care if he lives in China. Bring him on." We looked weak and afraid. In 1991, when I was elected Republican State Chairman, I took after Evan every week. I accused him of wasting our surplus ("Evan, where did the money go?") of buying Japanese equipment instead of good old USA equipment for the Highway Department, and everything else I could think of. Some of the charges against him, I just made up. Evan ran to Ed Lewis and questioned why Ed's friend was cutting him up. Ed explained that that's what the Republican State Chairman is supposed to do. Ed was a valuable advisor to Evan Bayh. There were a lot of monumental issues that happened on Evan's watch. The lottery, riverboats, the Beer Baron Bill, parimutuel racing, etc. The forces on both sides of these issues were powerful and influential, yet Evan was able to steer clear of any major problems.

The Governor, Clinton's Friend, and a Riverboat

One of the most interesting rumors concerned the riverboats. It was rumored that President Bill Clinton made a call to Governor Bayh and influenced one of the riverboat licenses. The license did go to some people in Kentucky who supposedly were friends of John Y. Brown, a friend of the Clintons. It was a little odd that there were no Hoosier investors in that license, especially when the one of the competitors for that particular license was a who's who of Hoosier Democrats, including the Simons. Who knows? Certainly not me.

Moose Turd Pie

It was interesting to note that all of the Riverboats that were licensed under Governor Evan Bayh had out of state ownership with a small percentage of the ownership giving to some Indiana Democrat operatives or contributors. The riverboats paid NO licensing fee, only a $50,000 application fee.

The race tracks that got permission to install slot machines at the tracks, in the 2007 legislative session, are 95% owned by home grown Hoosiers.

Ron Ratcliff, the majority owner of Hoosier Park is a lifelong Hoosier who lives in Lafayette, Indiana. Many of his investors are Lafayette natives.

Ross Mangano, the majority owner Indiana Downs, is a life long Hoosier, who lives in South Bend, Indiana where he manages The Oliver Trust (Oliver Tractor Family).

The licensing fee for the race tracks was $250 million for each track. Pennsylvania is $50 million and the Governor of Kentucky is going to propose a $50 million license fee.

It reminds me of when some of my pals went to Canada to hunt. No one wanted to cook. They cut cards, low man had to do all the cooking. The designated cook announced that anyone who bitched about the food would then become the new cook.

On the first night he cooked, one of the other hunters took a big bite of his supper and immediately spit it out. He said, WHAT IS THAT?" (meaning his supper).

The cook said "It's moose turd pie, why do you ask?"

The answer was "It's good – it's good".

A $250 million licensing fee: it's our moose turd pie. It's good – it's good.

(I have options that allow me to buy into the ownership of Indiana Downs.)

The Political Party of a Judge

I got a call one day from Steve Eichholtz, my pal Bob Eichholtz's oldest son. A municipal court judgeship was coming up, and Steve wanted the job. Steve asked me to introduce him to Ed Lewis. I arranged a lunch date for the three of us. Obviously, Steve wanted a recommendation from Ed Lewis to the governor, who would make the appointment. Now understand, even though the governor made those appointments, there was a statute that mandated the governor to appoint Republicans to certain courts. The judgeship that was open called for him to appoint a Democrat. Steve, like his father, was a card-carrying Democrat.

In about a month—surprise, surprise, surprise—Steve Eichholtz got appointed to the Municipal Court Bench. (I am sure Steve had other people also making recommendations to the governor.) In any event, a couple of months later, I got a call from Ed Lewis. He sounded out of sorts. He accused me of violating the rule. Ed said, "I get to pick the Democrats for jobs, and you get to recommend Republicans." I asked, "What are you talking about?" Ed said, "Eichholtz appointment." Ed thought Eichholtz was a Republican because he was a friend of mine. I loved it! You didn't get one over on Ed Lewis, even if it was an honest mistake. Ed passed in 1996, and a lot of people—including me—miss him. I am sure one of those who miss him is United States Senator Evan Bayh.

Chapter 24
Dan Quayle

When Edgar Whitcomb was elected in 1968, one of his young aides was Dan Quayle. There was a rumor that Dan had been assigned the job of inspecting the state's golf courses. In 1976, Dan Quayle ran and was elected to congress in the 4th District. He beat J. Edgar Roush, an entrenched Democrat incumbent.

The Great Big Reservoir

In 1977–1978, the Indianapolis Water Company, with Tom Moses as its president, saw the need for additional sources of water to accommodate a growing greater-Indianapolis. They decided to build a reservoir on Fall Creek at the northeast side of Indianapolis. They needed the U.S. Army Corps of Engineers' assistance, as well as other federal agencies.

The reservoir, of course, is Geist Reservoir. But what the water company wanted was a reservoir four or five times the size of Geist. It was to be called the Highland Reservoir. If original plans had been approved, much of what is now Fishers, Indiana would be underwater. This plan would also have required the purchase of thousands of acres with the help of eminent domain. Birch Bayh was the United States Senator from Indiana. Senator Bayh balked at the size and the eminent domain aspect and didn't sign off.

The Match

The fight was on. Moses got Frank McKinney, former Democrat National Chairman, to join his team. The Indianapolis Star was also supportive. Now Moses (a Democrat) and McKinney (a big Democrat) got into a pissing match with Birch Bayh. Of course, Bayh won that fight. We ended up with a much smaller reservoir.

The Payback

When it was time for Birch Bayh to run again, guess what? He had a strong opponent: Congressman Dan Quayle. Now not many gave Quayle a chance. I thought it was a kamikaze run. McKinney and Moses, and Eugene Pulliam, owner of The Star and Dan Quayle's grandfather, worked hard and called in some IOUs. Lo and behold, Dan Quayle beat Birch Bayh. I'm sure it didn't hurt anything that Eugene Pulliam, owner of The Star-News, was Dan Quayle's grandfather.

Unbelievable. As I've always said, paybacks are hell.

Chapter 25
Dave Caldwell,
THE *General*: Jack Dillon,
and Bob Eichholtz

Dave Caldwell

One of my best friends during the Dale Brown era was Dave Caldwell. Dave was an attorney who served in the legislature with me. Dave had been appointed by Dale Brown, the Marion County Young Republican Chairman.

Dave and his wife, Thelma, were home one Sunday morning when there was a knock at the door. It was Phil Wilke, who was running for Indiana Superintendent of Public Instruction. Phil Wilke was the son of Wendell Wilke, the Republican candidate for President who ran against Franklin Roosevelt. He was from Rushville, Indiana.

History and the Woman in the Car

Dave was a great student of Indiana history. He had a really good library, most of which were books about Indiana history. I am sure that David was interested in some of Phil's stories about his father and his Presidential race. Now

Phil had come to their door about 10 in the morning. Dave and Phil were deep in conversation as the time went on. About noon, Dave's wife (Thelma) announced to Dave that lunch was getting cold and that Dave should break up the conversation and eat lunch. Being polite, she invited Phil Wilke, and he accepted the invitation.

After lunch, there was coffee and dessert and more conversation. Finally about 1:30 that afternoon, Phil got up, thanked them profusely for lunch, and announced, "I have to be going as my wife Roselee is out in the car." It was a very hot and muggy day. Dave loved to tell that story.

Dave later was appointed to the Municipal Court Bench. He was a judge that the police, the defense lawyers, and the prosecutors liked. Very few judges are liked by all three of those groups.

Dave died at a very early age.

THE *General:* Jack Dillon

Another one of my Democrat buddies was Jack Dillon, "The General." He was the leader of our golf group. Dillon was by far the best player. He could shoot in the 70s about any time he wanted to, but he was also very stingy about giving up strokes. He had nicknames for all the guys in that group.

The Group and Their Names

One of them was Red Devil 13 (John Alden), a former Marine Corps pilot. The Good Aldini (Bob Alden), was his brother. False Face (John Domi) wore a wig. Bean Wop (Tony Benedict) was of Italian descent and played the soy bean futures in the commodities market. Hamburger Wop

(John Detillo) was also an Italian, but he owned several Wendy's. The Basement Judge was Jack Hesseldenz, who was the Center Township judge. The Left-handed, Ass-less Wonder was me. And we also had Ratis Ratis Immensis (the scientific name of the largest rat known to man, the great Indian wharf rat) who was from Crawfordsville and was a sort of a slow pay. There was Crazy, Kinky Kuntzie (Tom Kuntz), a local lawyer. Triple Hitch (Don Bates) was a sports writer for The Indianapolis Star. And, of course, there was The General himself. Jack, a Democrat, had been Attorney General as well as the Commanding General of the National Guard, 38th Division.

The betting and the competition were intense. There were days that if you wanted a friend, you'd better bring your dog. My wife said all of my friends in this group were half-wits. It was fun, and I hadn't laughed as much since the hogs tried to eat my little brother when I lived in Wheatland.

The Good Fellow Theory

Dillon invented the Good Fellow Theory. It went like this: If you asked Dillon for a political favor, he would always say, "Okay, I'll try." If whatever you asked for came true, Dillon would take the credit. If it didn't, Dillon would say, "You should have come to me sooner." When Tom Alsip was appointed judge, Dillon asked me about him. Dillon never heard of him. Said he'd never even heard the name. That afternoon we were playing golf, and Kuntz asked Dillon whether he knew the new judge. Dillon told Kuntz, "I'm responsible for him being appointed." Kuntz wanted the judge to hire him, Kuntz, as Public Defender. Dillon told

Kuntz, "Give me three strokes aside in our game today, and I'll do what I can for you." Kuntz gave him the six strokes. He lost all bets, and by sheer luck, was appointed Public Defender. He was grateful to Dillon thereafter. The Good Fellow had scored again. I played golf with Jack a few days before he died. He was playing poorly for Jack. He said he didn't feel good and thought he might have the flu. Three or four days later at Camp Grayling with the National Guard, Jack had a massive heart attack. If he had only gone to a doctor, it could have been averted. Jack Dillon was a great guy, and we all miss him.

Bob Eichholtz

Bob Eichholtz was a character; a 250-pounder who played football in the Navy and was on the all-Navy team. After serving in the Navy, he came home and was a great player for Tony Hinkle at Butler. Bob was the father of Judge Steve Eichholtz, Kurt Eichholtz, and the infamous Rickey Eichholtz of Ike & Jonesy's fame.

The Crazy Indian Theory

Among other things, my friend Bob taught me something that has been very important to me throughout my life. Bob called it the Crazy Indian Theory. Now according to Bob, when the Indians got old and became senile, they were treated with a great amount of respect by the rest of the tribe. Bob said they believed a spirit had invaded the old Indian's body.

The tribe would build the old Indiana a luxury tepee. They would situate it in the most sought-after spot. The old, senile Indian would yell and scream and threaten the other

Indians. The other Indians would react by leaving fish, buffalo meat, corn and pecan pies, and cheesecake, in front of the crazy Indian's tent.

No more wading around in cold streams trying to spear a fish; no more chasing buffalo all over hell's half-acre; nor more having to go to Marsh and get cheesecake. Everything was handed to them.

All they had to do if they ran out of something was to scream and yell obscenities and threaten the other Indians. What a sweet deal!

Bob was a master of the Crazy Indian Theory, and I adopted that early in my political career. It don't always work, but more often than not, it works.The Eichholtzes and the Earlys vacationed together when our children were young. We generally went to Hollywood, Florida and rented the cheapest place we could find.

Your Room Number, Please?

Bob had a habit of getting up early to walk the beach. After his walk, he went to Howard Johnson's for breakfast. Bob insisted that I join him. We ate a big breakfast, and Bob always insisted on picking up the check. Bob charged the check to a room number. The only problem was that we weren't staying there. I think Bob was singlehandedly responsible for restaurants demanding to see your key before charging something to a room.

The Man of Wars and the Men at Words

One morning, Bob and I were walking the beach. The lifeguard for that section of the beach was working on his informational blackboard, attached to his elevated stand.

The information on the board told the water temperature, when the high and low tides would be, the direction of the wind, and other like information. Now the day before, our six kids could not go in the water because the Man o' Wars were coming in on the ocean. A Man o' War is a jellyfish with long tentacles. If the tentacle touches you, it is very painful. I asked him, "Are the Man o' Wars coming in to-day?" He looked at me as if I fell out of the family tree. And he said, "The wind is from the west! The Man o' Wars float on top of the water. Now if the wind is from the west and the Man o' Wars float, how could they be in?" I said, "Do you mean the Man o' Wars actually live out in the ocean?" He asked, "Where do you think they live?" I said, "I thought they lived in them little condos like the rest of you smart alec assholes." Now this guy was big. He had some show-time abs, and he had a bad disposition. He took a couple of steps toward me. I jumped behind Eichholtz and gave him a finger so he would know I thought he was number one. Bob grunted and sucked in his gut, and all 250 pounds of him looked mean. The Hollywood lifeguard got back on his little chair.

Two Turkeys and Two Lobsters

Eichholtz was a hoot. We both shopped at a little store on Emerson Way. One day, our pal Owney Mullins—a great criminal attorney—was also shopping by himself. He had a list and wasn't paying much attention to anything but his list. When Owney was in the other aisle, Eichholtz put two Butterball turkeys and two live lobsters in Owney's cart. We watched while Owney checked his cart out and took every-thing home. We wondered what his wife said when he came home with two turkeys and two live lobsters!

Doc, Some Trees, and a Dog Named Brandy

Bob Eichholtz had a yard man who worked for him. His name was Doc, and he did all kinds of landscaping. Bob and I bought a bunch of trees from a nursery that gave us a good deal because it was late in the season.

One day that fall, Doc showed up at our house in his dilapidated pickup with a truckload of trees that he was going to plant for me.

Now the neighbors across the street had a very large St. Bernard dog with a ferocious bark. The dog's name was Brandy. When Doc got out of his truck, here came Brandy tearing across the road and my yard barking at Doc. Doc was scared, and he climbed up on top of the cab of his truck.

Mrs. Thompson, the owner of Brandy, came out of her house, yelling at Doc. She said "He won't hurt you. He has been castrated."

Doc yelled back, "I ain't worrying about him screwing me. I'm afraid he will bite me."

Bob passed at the age of 50, and I sure miss him. He was a hoot.

Chapter 26
Mike Maio

Mike Maio and I were in Las Vegas. Our luck had been bad, and both of us had a bad case of the "shorts." (We were short of money.) When I go out of town, I buy a newspaper and read the local news. I am a compulsive newspaper reader. While reading the Las Vegas paper, I saw a large ad that someone bought, advertising the loss of their pet cat. It was lost around the Desert Inn, where we were staying, and there was a $150 reward.

That Darn Cat

I showed the ad to Mike and suggested we find the cat. Mike thought that was a great idea but felt that because it was so hot outside, we should get more than the $150. There was a phone number in the ad, and Mike called it. Mike started out, "I've got the cat." I'm sure the owner was jubilant. Then Mike said, "It has torn my drapes and has soiled my good carpet. I've got to have $300 to pay for the damages." The man on the other end said, "You're the third con artist that's called today!" and he hung up. Mike was mad and rightly so. It was too hot to hunt for a $150 cat. Mike said the man was so rude that if he saw the cat, he would kill it.

The Ticket in the Bible

On his way to the Super Bowl in California, Jack Hesseldenz had stopped at Las Vegas. He made a pretty good bet on one of the teams at the Star Dust casino. His team won, and Jack had the ticket. I told Jack I was going to Vegas, and he asked whether I would cash his ticket and bring him back the money in Indianapolis. I said sure.

About the third day we were there, I figured I would go cash Jack's ticket. I was with Maio on this trip. I thought I would mess with Maio's mind a little. I called him in my room and showed him the ticket. I told him I had found it in the Gideon Bible in my room. I said I really don't know what it was. Mike looked at it and said it was a sports bet ticket. I said it was probably a losing ticket, and that's why someone had left it there. Mike looked at the ticket a while and said, "This is on the Super Bowl, and the bet is on the winner." I cautioned him that it just may be that it had been doctored or changed and that if I tried to cash it, they would think I did it.

We decided to would walk over there, and I would try to cash it, with Maio hanging back to get me out on bond if the ticket was a phony. I walked up to the window, gave the man the ticket, and he counted out $2,100 for the $1,100 bet Hesseldenz had made. Just as I knew he would. We walked out of the casino, and Maio was happy. He said, "I'm in for half." I asked him how he figured that, and he said because we had a two-bedroom suite, we should split things fifty-fifty. My theory was that I would keep everything I found in my room, and Maio should do the same. Maio gave me a little nod, and he said, "Okay, give me $500." I said no. It was my ticket, and I found it. I didn't tell him until we got home that it was Hesseldenz' ticket, which he gave to me to cash.

The Man Who Doesn't Read or Write Well

After the passing of Unigov, someone figured out that the number of package store liquor licenses had just increased. The licenses were selling for $30,000–$40,000 then. Keith Bulen's law partners (Charley Castor, Hank Dein, and Ted Robinette) were indicted as well as Jimmy James, who owned some existing liquor stores. All of them were later found not guilty in federal court by the Honorable Cale Holder.

Maio's father, Tony Maio, had been the Democrat County Chairman and some way, some how, the family corporation had gotten one of the licenses. Mike was subpoenaed before a federal grand jury. They asked Mike who his fellow stockholders were. Mike testified he didn't know who they were. The person asking the questions was irate. He said, "You own stock in a corporation, and you don't know your fellow stockholders? Mike said, "I own stock in General Motors, and I ain't got no idea who the other stockholders are."

Several years later, Mike was tried and found guilty of "insider trading" on the stock market. When asked questions, Mike claimed he didn't know how to read well enough to get much out of The Wall Street Journal, and he couldn't write real well, either. Mike and I coached CYO football together. We even won the city tournament. He was a character, who, under oath, claimed he really couldn't read or write.

Chapter 27
Federal Judge Al Sharp

In 1952, Richard Nixon was the Republican Vice President candidate, running on the Eisenhower ticket. In the fall of 1952, Richard Nixon campaigned in Indiana by traveling on a train across the state. Nixon spoke from the back of the train, along with Senator Bill Jenner and Congresswoman Cecil Harden, at Terre Haute. Three young men were in Terre Haute to hear Nixon speak: Al Sharp, Bill Maxum, and me. The three of us have been friends since that night, as our paths have crossed many times in politics.

The Judge and Bulen

In 1968, I got a call from Al Sharp. He was the elected Prosecutor for Warren County. He said that he wanted to run for the state office of Indiana Attorney General. He asked me to talk to L. Keith Bulen and try to get the Marion County support for him at the upcoming Republican convention.

I walked over to Bulen's office and made the request for his help. At that time, Marion County had about 220 delegates. Bulen said, "Forget it." He had made a deal to support Ted Sendak from Lake County, and he would not consider my pal, Sharp. Sharp did not like this answer and growled around, saying he would just run anyway. I told him he could count on one vote out of 220 from Marion County, and that one vote would be mine.

About two weeks later, I got another call from Sharp asking whether I would go back and ask Bulen about support if he ran for Judge of the Appellate Court at the convention. Bulen said he had no commitments for that judgeship and to come back in a week. I did, and Bulen said okay — to send Sharp in to meet him.

Bulen supported Sharp, and he was elected to the appellate court. Al served on the Appellate court with distinction. He was nominated for a federal judgeship with Bulen's endorsement, during the Nixon Presidency. The Senate concurred, and Al Sharp was appointed Federal Judge for the Northern District of Indiana by President Richard Nixon.

Al Sharp has the reputation of being a superb judge. I will always believe that he would have been appointed during the Reagan years to the U.S. Supreme Court. The thing that prevented that appointment was a marital problem that occurred when he was serving out of Lafayette. Al had been divorced, and he had married one of the employees of the federal court. Al later divorced her. She was bad news. She got in trouble and went to jail, which I found unusual for a federal judge's wife.

On the Way to Dinner

My wife and I were at Marco Island, Florida when we got a call from Al. He was in Naples and wanted to meet for dinner. He drove over to Marco. I was driving to the restaurant, and Al was telling a story. This is how the story started: "When my second wife was in jail..." I stomped on the brake, pulled to the side of the road, and told my wife, "You are listening to history." I can guarantee you that no federal judge from anywhere or at any time has ever started a story by saying, "When my second wife was in jail." Judge Sharp chastised me for those remarks, and we had a great dinner.

His reputation as a no-nonsense judge is well established. He had been a loyal friend of Bulen's even when Bulen was having problems. He believed in the rule, "Don't trade old friends for new ones". I am very proud to be his friend. He is a great man.

Chapter 28
A Friend in the Slammer

I have a friend named Art who had a little problem with the federal Securities and Exchange Commission (SEC) and did a couple of years at the Terre Haute. When he was first found guilty, he asked me to drive him over to the prison in Terre Haute because he didn't want his wife and his kids to have that experience. He was to report at high noon. At about 11:45, we pulled up in front of the prison. He said, and I quote, "I don't want you to get involved with this, so just drop me off." I was State Chairman at that time. I knew he was a little nervous, so I insisted that I go along. I parked and went in with him. We went into a glass waiting room. At exactly noon, a man who looked like the winner of the Yasser Arafat look-alike contest said, "Which one of you is Art?" Art pointed to me and said, "It's him!" The guard did not find this the least bit funny. I just hate people with no sense of humor.

As I said, I was on Art's visitors list the whole time he was at Terre Haute. And one time, I walked into the building, and I heard a voice say, "Rex! Rex!" I looked around, and there was another acquaintance, Doc. The rules were that you talk only to those people whose visitor list you're on, and I sure wasn't on Doc's list. But we exchanged pleasantries, and I asked him how he was doing. He said, "I'm doing just great. I love this f***ing place. I wish you'd use your political influence and get me a little more time." He had already served seven years. Doc also told me there were 485 inmates at Terre Haute, and he was the only guilty person there. Everyone but Doc, according to them, was not guilty!

Doc now runs a bar called Fatsos. It's on Oliver Avenue in Indianapolis. I am sure that Fatsos was the bar where they shot the bar scene in the Star Wars movie. The producers of Star Wars did not have to use actors dressed up like aliens. They just used the regulars who go there every day. Do not tell me there is no such thing as flying saucers and aliens. I've seen aliens at that bar. Fatsos is painted Colts blue. You can't miss it. (Do not leave anything of value in your car.)

Another one of the residents of Terre Haute at that time was a former prosecutor from Wayne County. He happened to be a Republican. I was the Republican State Chairman, and I would rather have been a little bit under the radar screen when I was going to visit somebody in prison. The former prosecutor, if a block away, would scream out, "Mr. Chairman! Mr. Chairman!" And of course, all of the permanent residents in there turned around to see who had just walked in. But anyway, there were no repercussions, and I really didn't care if there were. Art was my buddy. I felt like going over to visit him was the least I could do. I think someplace in the Bible it says you've gotta go visit people in jail. Lord, I did it.

Chapter 29
The Tricks of Winning Elections

Politics in the '70s and '80s was fun. One of the characters in the political arena at that time was a guy named Jim Cunningham. Jim was a Democrat. At one time, he had been the county sheriff. In the '60s and '70s, he was the Center Township Assessor. When he was assessor, his chief deputy's name was "Slick." That ought to give you some idea of how to get a favor out of the assessor's office. Jim was really the epitome of the old Irish Democrat. Even though we were on opposite sides, Jim and I were friends. He'd been there a long time, and he lived out in the neighborhood near where I was the Ward Chairman. He was a great guy. As the Democrats used to do, they had a factional fight. Cunningham was on one side, and Paul Cantwell (a former county commissioner and city councilman) was on the other. (Paul Cantwell's daughter, by the way, is the United States Senator now from the state of Washington.)

Will the Real James Cunningham Stand Up?

One year when Cunningham was running, Cantwell, who was opposing James Cunningham, found an elderly African-American gentleman—also named James Cunningham—and they talked him into running for Center Township Assessor in the primary against the real Jim Cunningham. So if you can imagine, there were two James C. Cunninghams running for assessor. Cantwell had yard signs made of the African-American Jim Cunningham sitting in a rocking chair, and he distributed those yard signs out in all the redneck precincts. The real Jim Cunningham won anyway.

Another time, "parties unknown" handed out $3 bills, with Jim's picture, implying that because Jim wasn't married—and he never was—that he was probably gay. They played a little rough in those days. Politics then wasn't "bean bag."

Same Voter, Different Hats

In one primary, my good friend Jack Hesseldenz was the Democrat precinct committeeman in the 9th Ward 5th Precinct, the same precinct where I was the Republican Precinct Committeeman. Jack was strong for Jim Cunningham, and Jack was working hard on that primary. The Republican slate didn't have opposition; the slate was going to carry on the Republican side, so I didn't really care what the Democrats did. It wasn't my business; I was looking out for the Republican side. I do remember though that Jack was busy hauling voters.

About 8 a.m., he brought in a voter wearing a straw hat. I noticed in the month of May that a big straw hat seemed a little odd, but because it was a Democrat voter, I didn't pay much attention. Jack brought the guy in and voted him. About 1 that afternoon, I noticed that he brought in a voter with a cowboy-type Stetson hat. I thought the man looked familiar. He voted, too. Then at 5 p.m., he brought in a voter with a leather aviator's helmet, complete with goggles, and I was sure I'd seen that voter before. And in respect for the integrity of the ballot box, I challenged my good friend Hessie and accused him of voting the same person three times probably by using names of people that Hessie knew were either deceased or had moved and were still on the voting list. Hessie sort of admitted as much but argued it was okay because the guy had changed hats.

Finally, Jim Cunningham got beat in the primary after many years of service, and I talked Bud Gohmann, who was a County Commissioner, into appointing Jim Cunningham to the Marion County Liquor Board. Bud's appointment, by law, had to be a Democrat. Two or three months later, Jim called me. He asked, "Why are you and Bud mad at me?" I told him we were not mad, and why he asked that. He explained that we had to be mad at him because he'd been on the liquor board for two or three months, and we hadn't once told him how to vote. You see, as I've always said, Democrats have more fun.

Chapter 30
The Stowing of
Absentee Ballots

This story is about an unnamed former friend I had. He borrowed $25,000 from me, and I haven't seen much of him since. But he was funny, and he was really a great story teller. He was a strong, conservative Republican. One time, I recruited him to work on the polls on Election Day. I had assigned him as a judge in a precinct in the 6th Ward, made up of predominately African-American voters.

The inspector really runs the polls on Election Day. This precinct inspector was brand-new; he'd never been an inspector before. He was an elderly gentleman, and he asked for help from my friend on certain things.

Sometime in the afternoon, a taxi pulled up, and they delivered the absentee ballots for that precinct, which was the normal way things were done then. They were given to the inspector. No one had told him during his instructions about the absentees. He asked my former friend what to do with the absentees. My former friend, realizing they were probably 100 percent Democrat votes, said, "Throw them away!" The inspector walked to the wastebasket and threw them away.

My former friend couldn't shut up about what happened. He loved telling that story. However, as luck would have it, there was talk of a recount. I ran into him a few days later, and I said, "Okay, wise guy, what are you going to tell them when questioned about the absentee ballots?" He said that he didn't say, "Throw them away". He said, "I said stow them away!"

Chapter 31
Jug Eckert and
the Hog Nuts Party

One of my best pals is Jug Eckert, a really big man with a really big heart. We are the same age. Jug grew up in Jasper, and I grew up in Vincennes, but we met in Indianapolis. Actually, we met one night in 1963 when my friend Bobby McKinney and I had a small car accident at 1 in the morning. Neither of us were hurt badly, but Bobby's car took a beating. Bobby called and woke up his friend, Jug Eckert. Jug had a wrecker to haul what was left of Bobby's car. Now Jug's disposition is sometime a little shaky at noon. At 2 in the morning, it's downright awful. Because it was a one-car accident, we saw no reason to bother the police.

Jug ran the Jasper Engine Exchange in Indianapolis. Soon after that, Jug bought a paneled truck, put some kitchen equipment in it, and went into the catering business. Jug was a great cook, and his food was good.

Jug's First Fundraiser
John Snyder was the Republican Chairman at that

time and was planning a fundraiser at the fairgrounds. Bill Buckley was the speaker. Bill Colbert was helping Snyder with the event, and I talked Colbert into hiring Jug to do the catering. We had chicken and fried biscuits, and it was good. The State Board of Health inspected us just before the dinner and made Jug and me wear hairnets. That was the first large political party that Jug catered.

This Chicken Smells Funny

Several years later, Jug and I both had children at Chatard High School. Jug's son, Zack, and my son, Pat, were on the football team. The parents' Athletic Booster Club decided to have a fundraiser to buy athletic equipment. Jug catered it for free, and the mothers were supposed to help. For that dinner, they bought whole chickens and cut them up. One mother grabbed a whole chicken, put it up to her face, and smelled it. She said, "Jug, this chicken smells funny." Jug said, "Ma'am, Miss America couldn't pass that test!"

Giving and Taking of Better-Tasting Food

Jug was always charitable to a fault. At any kind of a church or school function, Jug was there catering for free. The same with anything helping kids. To say that some took advantage of Jug would be a gross understatement. But I have heard Jug say, "The more things I do to help good causes, the more successful I've become."

I have watched as some of our community leaders ask Jug to cater a charitable event, and he would do it. Then when those leaders had a party, they hired another caterer. Jug had done yeoman's work in feeding the masses at the Pan Am Games. Soon after that, some of the same people who ran the Pan Am Games were putting on the PGA Golf Tournament at Crooked Stick. I'm sure Jug thought he would get a big catering job. Unlike the Pan Am Games, this would be a "get-paid-a-fair-price" job. The group hired a caterer from Louisville for the main tents and gave Jug a small part. The funny thing was, Jug's food was better. (I admit that I was the one who gave this information to the newspaper.)

Telling Turtle Stories

Jug and I were having a cocktail one day, and we started telling stories about big turtles we had caught. (Don't ask me why we were discussing that.) The next day, we took off toward Vincennes to my Number 1 Turtle hole in Marraha Creek. We set trout lines baited with chicken parts that Jug brought along, and just like I said we would, we caught a boat load of big turtles. Now what do we do? We will have a Turtle Stew Party. I had forgot how miserable it was to clean turtles. It's a messy job that on a hot, sunny day will attract green flies from out of state.

Jug had a great recipe for turtle stew, and we invited maybe 200 people. Because Jug and I are the same age and because my birthday is in July and Jug's birthday is in October, we labeled the gathering our birthday party.

A Thousand Pounds of Rocky Mountain Oysters

The next year, we decided to have another birthday party but not with turtle stew. At this one, we would serve Rocky Mountain Oysters, which some people call hog nuts. At the end, we bought 1,000 pounds of hog nuts, and they were a bitch to clean.

Keith Bratton drew up our invitations. In that first year with hog nuts, we sent 500 to my politician and business friends and Jug's friends. We continued that tradition for 18 years.

It's a Guy Thing

It was always a "stag party" although one year some of the political women dressed up like men and crashed the party. One of them looked like a man before she dressed up. We did have female bartenders, and because of the tips, we had plenty of volunteers. The party grew and grew.

The governors came, the legislators came, the judges, prosecutors, sheriffs, police, city council, state office holders, bookies, assorted gamblers, bonds men, con men, pimps, and lawyers. You name them, they were there. If you weren't at the party, you were a nobody.

Later on, we sent out 1,200 invitations, and 2,500 people would show up to eat hog nuts. Jugs had other appetizers and other Jug's food and free bars. Now hog nuts affect different people in different ways. Some said after eating hog nuts, they wanted to go home and make love in the mud.

Larry Conrad, a Democratic office holder and a great guy, loved it. This party was when Republicans and Democrats got together one afternoon and evening and actually liked each other and talked. Larry was always trying to promote that, and the Hog Nut Party was his dream event.

The number attending got out of hand. One year, in the invitations, we wrote, "If we had wanted your brother-in-law, we would have invited him." It didn't faze the crowd. Another year, we included a pass. Each person had to have a pass to get in. They counterfeited the passes.

One year, Jug got a call from a wife whose husband went to the party and didn't come home for two days. We always had the party at Dawson's Lake. When the parking lot filled up, people parked on Westfield Boulevard from Broad Ripple to 72nd Street.

One evening, we got a call from the sheriff's office. Because of complaints, we were to announce that all the cars parked on Westfield had to be moved, or they would be ticketed and towed. About that time, Jim Wells (the sheriff himself, and a guest) grabbed the microphone and said, "You can forget that last announcement."

Early Said Jug Made Him Do It

It all came to an end in 1991 when I became the Republican State Chairman. The party chair shouldn't be having parties that were stag only.

When I ran for governor, I knew I was going to have to take some heat about having stag parties. Sure enough, at a press question-and-answer session, Mary Beth Schneider and Mary Deeter were waiting. One of them said, "Rex, for years, you had a males-only party. Do you have something against women?" I was ready. I said no, I sort of like women, and for years I argued with Jug that we should invite women, but he wouldn't do it. That was a lie. But that ended that. Besides, Jug wasn't running for anything.

Chapter 32
The Politics of Cable Franchises

I got a call one day from a friend, Joe Areddy. Joe worked for Inland Container as their public relations and governmental relations man. At that time, Inland Container was a subsidiary of Time-Life. Time-Life also owned American Cablevision. American Cablevision wanted the Indianapolis franchise. Joe had been given the job by his boss at Inland Container to help American Cablevision get the franchise at Indianapolis. Joe needed help.

Rent a Civic Leader

American Cablevision was busy all over the country trying to get the lucrative cablevision franchises. Their modus operandi was to set up a separate corporate entity of which they would own 80 percent, and the local yokels would own 20 percent. Obviously, they wanted partners from the community who were well known and had some influence with the governing bodies that handed out the franchise.

This process was dubbed by the press as "Rent a Civic Leader." Because the governing body here was the City-County Council, Joe wanted me to help put together a group of Indianapolis people who might have some influence with the City-County Council.

The president of Inland Container had already asked some of his acquaintances to join this effort. The problem was that although the ones he picked were the high and mighty in the corporate world, none of them had a clue about the City-County Council. Some of the names who were already onboard were Otto Frenzel III, President of Merchants National Bank; Frank McKinney, Jr., President of American Fletcher National Bank; Al Stokely, from Stokley-Van Camp; Sarkes Tarzian from Bloomington; Lew Enkema; and Sam Sutphin. They were all community leaders, but I was not sure whether they were going to be a lot of help with the council.

I added some names who might not belong to Woodstock Country Club but who knew what a city councilman looked like (besides myself). My recommendations were Julia Carson, Pat Chavis, Larry Buell, Bill Crawford, Jack Dillon, Bob Eichholtz, Frank Otte, Ed Yates of the UAW, Margaret (Mrs. Alex) Clark, and Letha Rhea.

Other members were John B. Smith, Carl Dortch, Tom Hasbrook, P.E. McAllister, and Gene Sease, all of whom were well known in the community and also were or had been involved in the political arena. This was our "Rent a Civic Leader" team.

In addition to the American Cablevision group, there was another group competing for the franchise. That was Indianapolis Cablevision. They, too, were loaded for bear. Their general partners were Tom Binford, Art Angotti, Jim Ackerman, Eldon Campbell, Joe Dawson, Eddie French, and Kelley Robbins. In addition, they had as investors Bob

Borns, Hallie Bryant, Clarence Doninger, Dick DeBolt, F.C. Tucker, Dr. Frank Lloyd, Gordon St. Angelo, Glen Swisher, Dave Knall, Dick Petticrew, Gene Hibbes, and others.

Indianapolis Cablevision had a virtual platoon of heavy-weights. Needless to say, the winners would share a big payday, so the feelings ran high.

The Council Hands Out Two Cable Franchises

There were two franchises to be given away by the council. One was the area in Marion County outside the old city limits. The second was the old police and fire district, which was the old city limits, before Unigov.

The suburban area franchise was heard first by the council, and Indianapolis Cablevision was awarded the franchise. That franchise is now the area that Comcast serves.

The second hearing was for the franchise in the old city boundaries. That area is now served by Bright House. American Television was awarded that franchise, and we won by one vote.

The Indianapolis Cablevision franchise was later sold to Indianapolis Power & Light (IPL), which sold it to Comcast. I have no idea how their investors made out.

American Cablevision and the Negotiators

I do know that American Cablevision bought out the remaining Indianapolis partners in October of 1986. During the eight years from the time of their original investment, several of the investors sold their shares. Every year, American Cablevision gave us a buyout price, which was good for the year. It was usually a low-ball offer.

I always advised those selling to hang on, but some had

to sell for various reasons. Those that did stay the course were well rewarded. Gene Sease and I did the negotiations for the buyout, and we were good negotiators. I hadn't just got off the noon balloon from Rangoon, and I had a good idea what our shares were worth.

Besides that, American was negotiating with IPL to buy the franchise they owned. So they were under the gun to get our shares because there was a clause in our agreement that they could not dilute the value of our shares by increasing our debt. They were in a box. They bought our shares for a price of more than $80,000 per share.

I am not at liberty to say how many shares my partners had, but I had 11. Santy Claus came early to Rex's house that year. I was not like my pal in southern Indiana who hit the Hoosier Lottery. I saw him a year after he won one million dollars. He said he spent half of it on gambling, whiskey, and wild women, and then wasted the other half.

Chapter 33
Sophistisucks and Hully Gullys

Republican politics is made up of two kinds of people: sophistisucks and hully-gullys. It is important that you identify them as coming from one camp or the other. That is fairly easy. What is not easy is identifying the sophistigully and the hullysucks. They are half and half.

The Truth about Sophistisucks and Hully-Gullys

Sophistisucks: They will always wash their hands after they pee. Hully-gullys, on the other hand, are taught early on not to pee on their hands.

Sophistisucks usually belong to country clubs like Woodstock, Meridian Hills, or Crooked Stick. Hully-gullys play at Pleasant Run or Riverside.

Sophistisucks wear golf shorts that come exactly just below their knees, and they use new Titleist golf balls, even on water holes. Hully-gullys sometimes play with their shirts off and use X-out balls or balls they found in the water holes.

Sophistisucks drink things like Gray Goose. Hully-gullys drink Bud or Miller.

Sophistisucks go to Starbucks and spend three or four dollars on something called Mocha Grande. Hully-gullys go to White Castle for their coffee or at the Shell station where they sell Little Debbie cakes and Otis Spunkmeyer Cookies.

Now the real tests:

Sophistisucks, while talking to a hully-gully, will keep looking over their shoulder to see whether anyone more important is around. Hully-gullys are content to dance with who brung them.

Hard to Tell

One of the real litmus tests is whether they know who George Jones (The Possum) is and also know he served in the Marine Corps before he married Tammy. You can also question them to see whether they know when Dale Earnhardt, old #3, went to the great NASCAR race in the sky.

It's really had sometimes to classify even your friends. Mark Lubbers went to Harvard, but yet he claims to be a hully-gully. Hully Murray Clark went to Kenyon and rubs shoulders with Sophistisucks, but he is really 65 percent hully-gully.

Our governor went to Princeton and worked in the White House, but yet, at one time, he hung out at a place called the Alley Cat, rides a Harley, and eats two-pound tenderloins. He has to be at least 60 percent hully-gully.

John Dillon, Mike McDaniel, and Jim Purucker all have hully-gully qualities. Give them 80 percent.

Doug Brown, who has a great big boat and belongs to Woodstock, and Judge Frank Otte have some sophistisuck qualities but have a majority of hully-gully qualities. A narrow majority: 55 percent.

The Hully in Friends

Now most of my everyday friends are 100 percent hully-gullys: Bud Gohmann; Don Campbell; John White; John Gregg (a stone hully); Jim Clark; Jug Eckert; Mike McDaniel; Stan Strader; Art Belford; Larry Shuman; Gordon Tabor; and a couple from Vincennes, Jack Farmer and Duck Doyle, just to name a few. (A bunch of my really good friends are dead, but they were all hullys).

Duck and the Test

I will always remember my pal, Duck Doyle. Duck and I were in the same business math class in high school. To say that Duck was not a great student is an understatement. One day, Fred Alwood, our teacher, gave a pop quiz that we were to grade on the honor system. Fred gave the correct answers and then asked around the room to get their test scores. Some of our better students got a 90 or a 95. Duck announced he got a 100. Now Mr. Alwood had not come to town on a load of pumpkins. He asked Duck to bring his test up so he could see it.

Duck stood up and said, "I was just shitting you, Fred. I didn't even take it."

Fred said, "Donald, go to the principal's office!" We have been buddies ever since.

Chapter 34
Myrmidons and
Mummy-Dummys

I told you about sophistisucks and hully-gullys. You also need to know about myrmidons and mummy-dummys. Let's take mummy-dummys first because they are the least dangerous.

Mummy-Dummys

When Dale Brown was the Marion County Republican Chairman, he ate lunch every day at the Columbia Club. At about 11:45, three or four men gathered on the street at the stairwell. Dale walked down from his second-story office at Market and Pennsylvania. They lit his cigarette and made small-talk with Dale all the way to the Columbia Club. They didn't want anything other than the recognition of being seen with and talking to the great and the powerful. That's the example of an "extreme mummy-dummy." Other grades of mummy-dummys all laugh at the high-and-mighty's jokes. If asked, they always agree with what he or she says. They are satisfied with simple recognition.

Myrmidons

Myrmidons are different. They have an agenda. They have the same characteristics as mummy-dummys. They ingratiate themselves with the high-and-mighty, but don't you believe they are alike. They don't want recognition. They want money; they want power.

I'm here to tell you that government is a virtual gold mine for a good myrmidon. They tell the inexperienced that they are there "to help." What they really want is to help themselves to government or government agencies' contracts. If they are lawyers, they want the bond business. (All of government is constantly issuing or calling bonds.) Or they might just want their clients to be successful in dealing with government. I have seen some great myrmidons get filthy rich.

One of the main differences between myrmidons and mummy-dummys is that your mummy-dummys will come to your funeral. A successful myrmidons might come, but it will depend on the weather.

Chapter 35
The American Battle
Monuments Commission

The American Battle Monuments Commission (ABMC) is an independent agency of the Executive Branch. "It is responsible for commemorating the services of American forces where they have served since 1917 through erection of suitable memorial shrines and for designing, constructing, operating, and maintaining permanent American military burial grounds in foreign countries."

On January 14, 1982, I received a letter from President Reagan appointing me to the American Battle Monuments Commission. The main mission of the American Battle Monuments Commission is the care of our war-dead in foreign lands. I can tell you that this commission is fulfilling its mission and is certainly keeping the faith with our fallen heroes.

When World War II ended, 360,810 American men and women had died overseas. Most of them were buried near where they fell and were in temporary graves on alien soil.

In the years that followed, more than half were brought

back to their homeland at the request of their next of kin. All of those left in foreign soils now lie in permanent memorial cemeteries. Every family and next of kin was given the option for their fallen loved ones to be buried in our memorial cemeteries near where they had fallen. Or, the families could request their remains be returned to the United States.

I think the main reason for a family to choose that their loved ones be buried overseas was that, "They would have wanted to be buried with their 'comrades in arms'." I am sure that many who have served their country would understand this. General George Patton, a great American hero, is buried in our cemetery in Luxembourg. He told his family that he wanted to be buried with his troops.

World War I			
Cemetery	**Known Burials**	**Unknown Missing**	**Missing Commemorated**
Aisne-Marne, Belleau Woods, France	2,039	249	1,060
Brookwood, England	427	41	563
Flanders Field, Waregem, Belgium	347	21	43
Meuse-Argonne, Romagne, France	13,760	486	954
Oise-Aisne, F è re-en-Tardenois, France	5,415	597	241
St. Mihiel, Thiaucourt, France	4,036	117	284

World War I (Continued)			
Cemetery	Known Burials	Unknown Missing	Missing Commemorated
Somme, Bony, France	1,706	138	333
Suresnes (see also WWII), France	1,535	6	974
Totals	29,265	1,655	4,452

World War II			
Cemetery	Known Burials	Unknown Missing	Missing Commemorated
Ardennes, Neuville-en-Condroz, Belgium	4,530	783	462
Brittany, St. James, France	4,313	97	497
Cambridge, England	3,787	24	5,126
Epinal, France	5,186	69	424
Florence, Italy	4,189	213	1,409
Henri-Chapelle, Belgium	7,895	94	450
Lorraine, St. Avold, France	10,338	151	444
Luxembourg, Luxembourg City, Lux	4,975	101	370
Manila, Republic of the Philippines	13,464	3,744	36,280

World War II (Continued)			
Cemetery	Known Burials	Unknown Missing	Missing Commemorated
Netherlands, Margraten, Netherlands	8,195	106	1,722
Normandy, St. Laurent-sur-Mer, France	9,079	307	1,557
North Africa, Carthage, Tunisia	2,600	240	3,724
Rhone, Draguignan, France	799	62	293
Sicily-Rome, Nettuno, Italy	7,372	490	3,094
Suresnes (see also WWI), France		24	
East Coast Memorial, New York City, NY			4,596
Honolulu Memorial, Honolulu, Hawaii			18,094
West Coast Memorial, San Francisco, CA			413
Totals	86,722	6,505	78,955

For Those Who Could Be Named

The American Battle Monuments Commission has made each of our permanent cemeteries into a place of beauty and dignity. It was very emotional to stand at the entrance of one of our cemeteries and gaze at row after row of white marble headstones with a Star of David for those of the Jewish faith, a Latin cross for all others. Many buried there were 18 or 19 years old. When the name is known, the individual's name, rank, hisservice organization, his date of death, and his home state are inscribed.

For Those Who Couldn't Be Named

If the remains could not be identified, the inscription reads, "Here rests in Honored Glory a comrade in Arms Known But To God." In addition to the grave markers, there is also a Tablet of the Missing. It includes the names of those whose remains could not be identified as well as those lost and buried at sea, in addition to their names, rank, organization, home state, and the circumstances under which death occurred. I noticed that President Kennedy's brother, Joe, and Glenn Miller were on the Tablet of the Missing at Cambridge, England.

Emotions of Home

When our party arrived at a cemetery, I was given a list and the location of those buried or missing from Indiana. The list also included their hometown. Having grown up mostly in Vincennes, I recognized several families' names who had loved ones buried in that cemetery. That, too, was emotional.

Many of the graves have been "adopted" by the townspeople nearby. They bring flowers and decorate the graves in recognition of the sacrifices our boys had given for their freedom.

Our cemeteries' sites on foreign soil were granted in perpetuity by the host government free of cost, rent, and taxation. All of our superintendents are Americans.

WWI and WWII

The World War I cemeteries were built and maintained by the United States Department of War until 1934, when they were turned over to the American Battle Monuments Commission. General John J. "Black Jack" Pershing stayed in Europe after the war was over to make sure that the eight cemeteries where his men were buried were being taken care of.

Our World War II cemeteries all included a devotional chapel and a battle map or verbal history of the combat that was close by.

Do Not Dishonor Dead Soldiers

The superintendent of one of the WWI cemeteries told me this story. During World War II, German soldiers were stationed near our WWI cemetery. One night in the town, after too much beer, the German soldiers decided to visit the WWI cemetery and tear down all the Star of David monuments. That they did. Their commanding officer, after hearing this, sent them and others back to the cemetery to repair the damage and apologize. He was probably punished by his Nazi superiors later on.

As a member of the commission, I inspected almost all of our overseas cemeteries. We could not go to Carthage, Tunisia, or the Philippines because of "unrest" at that time in those countries.

How Rex Got Appointed

I sent my resume and a letter requesting to be appointed to the American Battle Monuments Commission. I had been told about the ABMC, and I also read about it in the Plum Book. (The Plum Book had a list of all the President's appointments and had a plum-colored cover.)

Keith Bulen and Gordon Tabor were both in Washington, DC. Keith was a member of the transition team, and Gordon Tabor had gone to assist Keith. I am sure both helped to make sure that my name and request were in the "computer."

I never really thanked Keith adequately for my appointment, but I am sure that without him and Gordon, this highlight of my life would have never happened. I am sure Keith knew how much I appreciated his help.

In the 1980 election, I had been the State Campaign Director for the Reagan team as well as the Marion County Reagan Chairman.

In May of 1980, I had Governor Reagan and Nancy at our home for a Sunday afternoon fundraiser, which I have written about.

A few months after the election, I was being roasted by the Indianapolis Press Club. Also being roasted was Lynn Nofsinger. He was Reagan's Press Director, as well as advisor and best friend. I remembered Lynn from a couple meetings we attended after the 1976 election. I reminded him of the meeting we had in Columbus, Ohio, and one in Chicago during a snowstorm. I also reminded him that we, in Indiana, carried Reagan in the primary against a sitting President, President Ford, in the '76 primary.

I told him about my request to be on the ABMC and how I got a letter back from Jim Baker thanking me for my request. Baker had not been for Reagan for President. He was running the show for George H. W. Bush. I knew that Lynn Nofsinger did not like Baker and resented the fact that Baker had "taken over." Lynn promised to chase down my paperwork and see what he could do when we got back to Washington. Soon after that, I got a letter of appointment from President Reagan. The Crazy Indiana Theory worked again.

The First Commission Dinner and Introductions

Within a few weeks, I got a letter from General Mark Clark, the Chairman of the American Battle Monument Commission. He set our first meeting date and invited all of the newly appointed Commission members to a dinner (the night before the meeting) that he was hosting at Fort McNair, near Washington. When I got to the dinner that evening, I must admit that I was intimidated. Now I'm not smart enough to be intimidated a whole bunch, but I was intimidated. Everybody there was obviously important.

General Clark, in greeting me, had done his homework. He knew I was in the Marine Corps, and he knew a lot about Indianapolis. It seems that prior to World War II, Clark was stationed in Indianapolis. His children went to Shortridge High School, and he was a member of the Indianapolis Masonic Lodge and the Scottish Rite Cathedral in Indianapolis. His first wife, deceased, was from Muncie; and his then current wife, Mary, was also from Muncie. He told me he was very close to the Ball family, and he had thought about retiring before the war and going to work for Ball brothers. One of the Balls had served with General Clark as his attaché during the Italian campaign.

After the war, General Clark was president of The Citadel and was a very thoughtful and kind person. He was truly one of America's heroes, and I grew to really like General Clark.

In addition to General Clark, there was Mrs. Omar Bradley, wife of General Omar Bradley, who was deceased. Also in the ABMC was General Ed Wheeler, a Vietnam hero, who should have been the Commandant of the Marine Corps. He was on the wrong side when some of the generals wanted to make Boot Camp more "'user friendly" and did for a while. Wheeler did not agree with that.

The other new members were either friends of the President or Vice President, or part of his campaign team. The Secretary of the ABMC was General Adams. In addition to the members, our staff was made up of people who were all Army colonels.

I mentioned that I was a little intimidated. As time went on that evening, I got to thinking that someone didn't realize that I had only been a sergeant, and a hully-gully at that.

The Toast

We sat down for dinner, and I was sort of hunkering down at the table. Didn't want to be too conspicuous, as they might ask me to leave. Almost immediately, one of the women, who had a death grip on the international facelift record, (one more face lift, and she would have a little goatee) stood up and proposed a toast to the best friend of her dear, departed husband. That, of course, was General Clark. Her toast was lengthy.

There Goes the Tablecloth

When she finished, General Clark stood up and proposed a toast to his great friend and mentor, General Omar Bradley. Now Mrs. Clark, Mary, had probably had a cocktail or two before arriving, and she might have had a cocktail or two while she was there. In any event, right in the middle of General Clark's Toast, Mary fell off her chair to the floor. She not only fell, but she took the table cloth, the salads, and the salad dressings with her. The general, after seeing she was not injured, went right along with the toast.

Just Like Home

Now all at once, I felt a lot better. Mary Clark falling off her chair was just like something that might happen in Vincennes. I began to sit up straight and become one of the crowd. God bless Mary. You don't reckon that Mary, a Hoosier, might have done that on purpose just to make me feel at home?

The Inspection Team

Our job as commissioners was to inspect and make sure our cemeteries and monuments were well kept. On inspection trips, we teamed up with another commissioner when we went overseas. I teamed up with Francis "Red" Bagnell, an all American football player who had won the Overland Trophy. Red was president of the College Football Hall of Fame. He was also close to, and a business partner with, George H. W. Bush, the Vice President. At the Republican National Convention in 1988 at New Orleans, I noticed Red and his wife sitting in George H. W.'s box.

The Celebration: We're Not in Wheatland Anymore

While I was on the ABMC, we celebrated the 40th anniversary of the Liberation of Rome and the 40th anniversary of D-Day. The entire commission was invited to go to these two celebrations.

We were transported to Rome on an Air Force "Special Mission Aircraft." It was somewhat like the President or Vice President's aircraft. We had a chef, two crews, sleeping quarters—you name it. From a double-holer in Wheatland to this: WOW! Freddie the Rat would have been proud.

We started in Italy, where we visited our cemetery near Angio Beach. In recognition of the 40th anniversary of the Liberation of Rome, we were wined and dined. Our ambassador to Italy, Ambassador Robb, had a dinner party at his residence. The embassy had a ceremony and party.

The Italian government had a reception with the President of Italy and the Prime Minister in attendance. The Mayor of Rome had a party. Our military attaché had a reception. There were other celebrations and receptions.

Bob Dole was in attendance representing President Reagan, as well as the Secretary of the Army John Marsh and the Chairman of the Joint Chiefs of Staff General Vessey.

A neat thing happened at the embassy reception. We had assigned seating, and I sat next to General Joe Lutz, who was head of the Delta Force. We struck up a conversation, and I told him that Jack Hesseldenz, O.B. O'Brien, and John White, all friends of mine, had said, "Hello." They were also friends of his. General Lutz was a graduate of Cathedral High School, where he was a great high school athlete. He and I really got a big kick talking about Indianapolis and our mutual friends.

General Donaldson

After the Rome ceremonies, we flew to Paris. Our European headquarters is in Paris, and General John Donaldson was our officer in charge. General Donaldson had an interesting background. He is a West Point grad and an Olympic medal winner. He was one of the "chosen ones" to advance in rank. In Vietnam, he was one of our top generals. There was talk of him being on the Joint Chiefs of Staff. He was a remarkable individual.

While General Donaldson was in Vietnam, the Mi Li Massacre occurred. Lt. Calley, and his men, supposedly wiped out a village that included women and children. Calley's defense was that he was in a fire-fight with North Vietnam in the village. Calley was found guilty by a court marshal.

Although General Donaldson was light years away from Mi Li, the buck stopped with him. General Donaldson got a reprimanded in his record book, and his chances for advancement were over.

We traveled from Paris to the Normandy area. We stayed at a neat chateau where the only other person besides us staying there was Walter Cronkite. He was not a friendly person.

Come June 6—D-Day—we were assigned a military Hughey helicopter that took us to our destinations. The ABMC was split up between ceremonies at Utah Beach, Omaha Beach, and Pointe du Hoc. The only person that got to move was President Reagan.

I drew Pointe du Hoc, and I was a little disappointed because at Utah Beach, the ceremonies would include the

Queen of England, Margaret Thatcher, Mitterrand, Trudeau, the Queen of the Netherlands, the King of Belgium, etc.

Heroes at Pointe du Hoc

As it turned out, Pointe du Hoc was the place to be. Pointe du Hoc was a high cliff overlooking both Omaha Beach and Utah Beach. At Pointe du Hoc, those fearless rangers who scaled the cliff to spike the German guns were there. Most of them who were alive made the trip.

They had a party the night before at one of the local pubs, and they invited the ABMC commissioners. They were stronger than a well rope. They were stronger than a garlic malt. It was a great party, and they were still tough. Party or not, the next morning and afternoon, they all sat at the top of Pointe du Hoc.

When the ceremonies started, President Reagan flew in by helicopter to Pointe du Hoc. Those brave survivors of 40 years before fell out into ranks, and the President walked down their lines shaking hands and talking to each one individually. Some were represented by one of their children, or their wives.

Forty years before 225 of our country's best started scaling the 100-foot–high cliff. They fired rocket-propelled grappling hooks to the top of the cliff and climbed up ropes to the top.

It was known that the Germans had six 155mm guns in thick concrete emplacements. Pointe du Hoc overlooked both Omaha Beach and Utah Beach. They could have massacred countless troops and ships.

The Rangers climbed and fought to the top despite

withering machine gun and rifle fire being fired down straight in their faces. Out of 225 who started the climb, 90 made it to the top where they killed the heavily fortified Germans.

President Reagan gave his best speech ever that day. With tears in his eyes, he praised and thanked the boys of Pointe du Hoc. Our three commissioners were seated in front, and I was probably five yards away from President Reagan. What an experience and honor to party, meet, and talk to the Rangers and then see and hear our all-time, best President.

What a lucky break I had. I do worry and fret that my grandchildren will never be taught about our nation's heroes. The "role models" for our children and grandchildren seem to be some 7-foot freak who can shoot a basketball, or can run the football, or hit a drug-induced home run.

The heroes of WWII were my heroes when I was growing up. The Sullivan brothers, the Marines at Iwo Jima and Guadalcanal, and Chuck Yeager. I must have watched the movie of John Wayne storming the beaches of Iwo Jima twenty times. The men and women we have serving in Afghanistan and Iraq are just as good as their predecessors, but a vast majority of Americans don't know it or don't care. Freedom ain't free.

I went to the War Memorial a while back to honor some of our current heroes, and there were maybe 100 people there. Shame on us.

I want to commend Brian Bosma who shows up at most of these ceremonies. Brian's father, Charley, served in WWII.

Also, Governor Daniels makes himself available for

many of these functions. I wish we had more office holders and just plain citizens come to the patriotic gatherings that thank our troops. I guess people are just too busy enjoying their freedom.

I think that every young person should have to spend two years of service for our country. (It would help solve our crime problem.)

Also, every school child in the state of Indiana should visit the Medal of honor Memorial in Indianapolis and listen to those brave men's sacrifices for their duty to their country, a sentiment that's not much in fashion anymore.

Chapter 36
The Indiana Society of Chicago

My first Indiana Society trip to Chicago was in 1962. I was invited by the lobbyist for the railroads at the Indiana General Assembly. We went by train to Chicago on Friday, and then attended the Society dinner on Saturday evening. We returned home late Sunday. Back then, the Indiana Society was male only. Now that was fun. Most of the legislators, political party leaders, lobbyists, the governor, and usually the senators attended. Many of the business leaders throughout the state were also in attendance.

The Guys' Night Out

One Saturday evening, I left the Society dinner a little early so I could get a cab and get back to my hotel before the crowd came out. A cab was parked there with a sign in the window reading Out of Service. One of my friends, Bill Schmadeke, came out soon after me and got in that cab. The driver, who spoke very little English, tried to tell my friend that his cab was out of service. My friend was irate and would not accept the out-of-service story. An argument ensued between him and the cab driver. My friend, all 6'5" of him, kicked the cab and bent the fender. The five-foot-six-inch cab driver took offense at that, and the fight was on.

My razor-sharp mind realized there was a problem. The problem was that the five-foot-six-inch cab driver was pounding my six-and-a-half-foot friend. I was in the process of trying to pull the cab driver off my friend, when another friend, Darrell French, came out to get a cab. Now Darrell, always the peacemaker, joined with me in trying to save Schmadeke's life by helping me get the cab driver off our friend. After we rescued Schmadeke, all three of us hailed another cab and headed for our hotel.

Cab number one with the bent fender was in hot pursuit. When we got to our hotel, not only was the first cab driver there, but so were the Chicago police. Now I, being a witness to the whole proceedings, tried to explain to the police how this five-and-a-half-foot cab driver, without provocation, attacked the six-foot-six-inch Mr. Schmadeke. I don't think he believed me because he said all three of us—French, Schmadeke, and me—should get in a police car and go to the police station. I felt we were about getting everything straightened out when Bill Schrieber (the Marion County Democrat Chairman) and Claude Magnason, arrived at the police station. They had heard about our plight and the insane cab driver, and had come to rescue us.

Schrieber introduced himself to the nice policemen and said if they didn't release us, he was calling Mayor Daley, who was a close friend of his. Because it was about 2 in the morning, that did not impress the policemen. Things were looking pretty bleak when another attorney, Jim Clark, our buddy, showed up. At the same time, the manager of the cab company arrived. Mr. Clark, a fast-thinking fellow, asked whether he and the cab company manager could meet in private. Mr. Clark was so convincing that the cab company manager went over to his driver and said, "You were wrong." Now the cab driver had lost a whole night's work and had a bent fender on his cab. But he was wrong? I guess justice prevailed, and the cab company manager probably showed up the next day in a new suit with some new pointed-toe shoes.

Frank's Business Cards and the Phone Calls

It was customary that the Saturday night Society dinner be sponsored by one of the large Indiana businesses. One year, American Fletcher National Bank was the sponsor. The sponsor also had some small table gift at each setting. Frank McKinney, Jr. was Chairman of the Board of American Fletcher. The table gift was a very nice metal business card case, and in each of the card cases, was Frank McKinney's business card, complete with his direct telephone number. Now in those days, over 1,000 people attended the dinner, and I must say that I'm sorry about the conduct of some of the people who were there.

I heard that starting the next week Mr. McKinney had numerous calls from cocktail waitresses and assorted other ladies of the night from Rush Street. They had been given Frank's card with the instructions to give him a call sometime, and they might even be considered for a job. What a rotten, dirty trick to give out Mr. McKinney's card with those instructions! Frank was a friend of mine, and I hope he saw the humor, but I doubt it.

The Republican Chairman and the Democratic Governor in the Corner

Several years ago, the Indiana Society weekend turned into a weekend to bring your family and do a little Christmas shopping. (It's always the first Saturday in December.) Also several years ago, women were invited to the dinner, and many of them attend.

At a private party on Friday night, I ran into Governor Bayh. It seems my pal, Judge Jan Downer, who was a municipal court judge, had rubbed some of the lawyers the wrong way. Judge Downer knew the law and was honest and fair, but his people skills were not the best. A group got together and asked the governor not to reappoint him. The day before the aforementioned party, someone in the governor's office had told some friends that Downer was out. He would not be reappointed.

The word spread even though the governor's appointments wouldn't be announced until the next week. As I was leaving, I said to Governor Bayh, "I hope you won't be too hard on my friend, Jan Downer." Evan said, "I want to talk to you about that." We went over in a corner, and I gave him my opinion. Judge Downer was honest and fair and knew the law, but he irritated some of the attorneys because of his demeanor, or so I told the governor. There was some speculation that night on why the Republican State Chairman and the Democrat governor were in the corner of the room in deep discussion.

I must have made my point. Evan reappointed Judge Downer the following week.

The Indiana Society weekend was, and still is, a great place to see and talk to people. At least it worked for Judge Jan Downer.

Chapter 37
The Indianapolis Foundation

I served on the Board of Trustees of The Indianapolis Foundation for 24 years. It was a gratifying experience and a great honor. The board is made up of six people, two appointed by the mayor, two by the Marion County Circuit Court Judge, and two by the senior federal judge. I was appointed in 1980 and served until December of 2004. The people who served before me were a Who's Who: Eli Lilly, Paul McNutt, Gustave Efroymson, etc…

A New Chairman
I had the great privilege of serving with Robert Efroymson and Dan Efroymson. Mr. Robert Efroymson, a great gentleman, really ran the Foundation from a policy standpoint. Robert and Dan, who followed him, both were very charitable people who were dedicated to improving the quality of life for those less fortunate. When I joined the Foundation, Robert Efroymson had been the permanent chairman. Jack Dillon, my pal, was also on the board and suggested that the chairmanship be passed around. Mr. Efroymson agreed. I was chairman for three different terms.

The Process

When I joined the board, we had around 36 million dollars, all of which were unrestricted funds. I understand that the Foundation today manages over 675 million dollars, most of which is restricted or donor-advised. Basically, we received requests from, or heard of, a non-profit that was doing good work and needed help—most of the time, the kinds of organizations that slipped through the cracks as far as United Way funding was concerned. We made a substantial gift to United Way, too, on an annual basis.

Corporate Pet Peeve

Our money came from bequests and gifts, mostly from Marion County residents who had accumulated wealth and wanted to give to worthwhile, charitable causes. They entrusted the Foundation to pick out those causes that needed help. Robert Efroymson's pet peeve was community leaders who donated to the Foundation from their corporation. Robert's point was that the community leader was not giving his money to charity: He was giving his stockholder's money. It was great to get the corporate money, but that didn't mean the CEO got "stars in his crown."

Dan Efroymson

Robert Efroymson was very kind to me and gave me a great compliment. He said he was glad that I took my responsibility very seriously and that I cared about people. He made the assessment after I had been on the board one year. Dan Efroymson took Robert's place on the board when Robert died. Dan was a great asset and one of the smartest people I had ever met. Despite his wealth, Dan was a Navy pilot who served his country by landing jets on an aircraft carrier. Dan was not only smart, but he had guts. After Dan's early death, the Efroymson family gave the Foundation in excess of 100 million dollars.

Faith-Based Grants

The only time Robert and I ever disagreed was about giving money to faith-based organizations. My belief was that some homeless person who was hungry wasn't going to be hurt if he had to say or listen to a little prayer in order to have a warm place to sleep or get something to eat. Besides, I felt the faith-based organizations do a better job. The policy was gradually changed, and my favorite organizations like the Little Sisters of the Poor, Seeds of Hope, St. Mary's Child Center, Wheeler Mission Ministries, and many more got grants.

Changes

My last few years on the board saw a lot of changes. We changed our name to the Central Indiana Community Foundation. Also, it seemed to me that our new policy had sort of shifted from strictly helping people to community-building. Also, I didn't agree that the Foundation be in the forefront of social engineering. I really was not in agreement with a grant of discretionary funds, even though it were only $1,000 to pay for Richard Florida to come to Indianapolis to speak. I don't agree with Richard Florida, who advocates that cities with a large "gay" community are better off economically and attract new innovative businesses. I have always felt that people can do whatever rocks their boat, as long as they don't do it in the street and scare the horses.

But regardless of an individual's feelings about some of the social issues of today, I don't think it's something the Foundation should be promoting. After all, we are spending other people's money.

The Foundation has done a great job of managing our grantors' money. The Investment Committee is the best ever assembled. We have beaten all the community foundations in the nation when it comes to money management. At the same time, the Foundation has awarded 118 million dollars in grants over the past five years.

I am sure the Foundation will continue to be a great asset of central Indiana. And the fact that I disagree with people don't make me right. Remember: It's a mighty thin pancake that don't have two sides.

I am always sure and often wrong.

Chapter 38
Vincennes University

Ed Whitcomb was elected governor in 1968. My friend, Bob Brown, was his law partner in Seymour. I worked on his campaign, actually running the Whitcomb Headquarters for several weeks. Don Tabbert was Whitcomb's campaign manager, but he got busy in a federal criminal trial defending a former Republican legislator. After Whitcomb was elected governor, I asked for and received an appointment to the Board of Trustees at Vincennes University. (I had attended Vincennes University.)

Vincennes University History

Vincennes University has an interesting history. In 1801, William Henry Harrison was appointed the first Governor of the Indiana Territory. That year, Harrison helped organize Jefferson Academy, which was the forerunner of Vincennes University. The trustees, besides Harrison (who was Chairman of the Board), were John Gibson, William Clarke, Henry Vanderburgh, and Frances Vigo. All had counties named for them.

In 1804, the Secretary of the Treasury designated 23,040 acres of ground, in what is now Gibson County, as a land grant to support the school. In 1806, Vincennes University was incorporated and given permission to take over Jefferson Academy, along with the 23,040 acres of ground. The board of Jefferson Academy became the board of Vincennes University with the addition on the board of Benjamin Parke (the first U.S. District judge) and Walter Taylor (one of the first two U.S. Senators from Indiana).

Now comes the good part. After Vincennes University was formed, they hired a young lawyer as the clerk of Vincennes University. His name was Jonathon Jennings, who later became the first Governor of the State of Indiana. William Henry Harrison did not like Jennings. (He was a lawyer, wasn't he?) And Jennings didn't like Harrison. At that time, Vincennes University had a lottery to help with its finances. Harrison claimed that Jennings "moogie-foogied" (my term) with the money from the lottery. (See? We had gambling in Indiana in 1806.) Jennings was either fired, or he quit. (He was hotter than a Jap.) Jennings then moved from Vincennes to Clarksville. He was elected as Indiana's first governor in 1816.

The Long Road without a Turn

Now I've always believed that "what goes around, comes around;" or, to put it another way, "it's a long road without a turn." And so did Jennings. Paybacks are hell, and Jennings paid Vincennes University back. As governor, he established the Indiana Seminary in Bloomington. The same year, the Indiana Legislature passed a bill that named an agent to "collect rents and profits" from the Vincennes

University land-grant ground. In 1822, the legislature went a step further and ordered all the Vincennes University land sold, and the proceeds were given to the state seminary in Bloomington, soon to become Indiana University. (I have researched this, and I don't think Bob Garton was in the legislature at the time.)

After numerous lawsuits filed by Vincennes University, Vincennes University received $30,000 from the state in 1846. In 1855, the legislature gave Vincennes University $66,000 for their loss of the land; and in 1907, the legislature gave Vincennes University another $120,000. All of this was done because of the state taking away Vincennes University's ground.

Tecumseh and Little Turtle's Betrayal

Another interesting fact about Vincennes University is that the campus is contiguous to Walnut Grove, which was the site of the historical pow-wow between the Indian chief and great warrior, Tecumseh, and William Henry Harrison.

Tecumseh traveled south on the Wabash River along with 300 of his most trusted braves for the meeting. During their meeting, it looked like they were going to go to war, but sounder heads prevailed. The Indians got screwed without even a kiss, when a lesser chief named Little Turtle gave away the farm in the Treaty of Fort Wayne. Tecumseh's trip and the meeting were brought about by Tecumseh trying to get the Treaty of Fort Wayne negated. Little Turtle had sold them out, and they knew it, but Harrison wouldn't budge. Little Turtle betrayed his own people, and that's why today hardly anyone names their kids "Little Turtle."

Hard Times

The years passed, and Vincennes University struggled to keep its doors open. Just think of the consequences. If there weren't a Vincennes University, would there have been a John Gregg (from Sandborn, Indiana, who was Speaker of the House and later, President of Vincennes University) or Rex Early? Scary, isn't it? Vincennes University was neither fish nor fowl. It was not really a state school nor a school connected with any religious denomination. Somehow, though, the university survived. In 1923, the legislature passed a bill that empowered the Knox County Council to levy a five-cent per one-hundred-dollar tax for the support of Vincennes University.

In 1955, State Senator Matt Welsh got a bill through the legislature that mandated the state to double whatever the Knox County levy produced and to give those funds to support Vincennes University. When I went on the board in 1970, I was one of 24 trustees. The governor got six appointments, and the other 18 were sort of self-appointed. These included most of the county's doctors and successful businessmen. Actually, Dr. Isaac Beckes, the Vincennes University President, set the agenda. He had a small executive committee to approve it. They ran it past the rest of the trustees after it was a done deal. Isaac Beckes was a Presbyterian preacher. He was a good person and very aggressive. He would make Vincennes University grow at any cost. A fiscal expert he was not. He was the eternal optimist. Whatever he did to keep Vincennes University going and making it grow was okay, it would turn out good. And grow we did.

Unfortunately, our income stream was not keeping up

with our growth. Isaac recruited some good people. To get good administrators and faculty, his sales pitch was that he couldn't pay top dollar, so he substituted that with tenure. Finally, Matt Welsh and I had a meeting and decided that we would recruit a fiscal officer because our financial situation was deteriorating. Matt and I tried to hire Red Taylor, who had been Governor Whitcomb's budget director. We offered him the title of Vice President of Finance and baseball coach. I knew the baseball coach thing would interest him, and it did. But I don't think his family wanted to move to Vincennes.

We hired one of Taylor's assistants and the person whom Taylor recommended, Bob Stryzenski. A short time after that, Dr. Beckes had a message for us at the Trustees meeting. We were broke. Busted. Tapped out. Whatever. We were out of money. The General Fund had a deficit of 3 million dollars. This was a lot of money in 1975. In addition to that, checks had been written to vendors but were never sent because of the cash-flow problem. Also, we had loans at both Vincennes banks, and we also spent some of our bond retirement funds. A real no-no.

There was no hint of impropriety nor any money missing. We had a "cigar box" accounting system, and because of the rapid growth, we ran out of money. In November, 1975, Dr. Beckes, Bob Green, Sr., Matt Welsh, and I met with a legislative task force where we laid out our situation and asked for help. Despite our financial situation, we were still the most affordable school in the state, and we were turning out a lot of Hoosiers with employable skills, and with transferable hours to our state's four-year institutions. Also, southwestern Indiana was underserved as far as postsecondary education was concerned.

The Bail Out

Needless to say, the legislators were not happy campers. They bailed us out with cash to pay the bills and a healthy appropriation of over 5 million dollars in the next budget. Some of their caveats were that we had to cut our board from 20 to 10 and that the governor would make the board appointments. And we would be like the other state-supported institutions, such as Indiana University, Purdue, Ball State, and Indiana State.

After the bail out, I got a call from Doc Bowen to come to his office. He wanted to discuss the appointment of the trustees. He said he wanted Lynn Gee, from Marshall County and a former native of Davis County, and me to be on the board, and he wanted my recommendations for the other eight.

My first recommendation was Matt Welsh, the former governor. Doc agreed. I also recommended a Republican businessman who owned a large business in Davis County who had been on our board. I was sure that Doc would want him, but Doc said no. It seems that Doc remembered his contribution to Doc's campaign, and it was obviously pretty pitiful.

Soon after that, Dr. Beckes retired, and we picked Phil Summers, who was on the Vincennes University staff, as our next president.

Back in the Day

I always had a feeling that Beckes remembered when I was a student there. I was an avid hunter and fisherman. During hunting season, I wore my hunting clothes to morning classes and brought my hound dogs to school. I tied them to the bumper of my car when I was in class. Any time a train went by, seeing as how the railroad was close to the campus, my beagle hounds howled. Also, my buddy (Harold) and I were accused of taking live 'possums to school and turning them loose. We pleaded no contest. The cover of the Vincennes University school paper, showed a character talking to Dr. Beckes while holding a possum—and they identified that person as me.

I want you to remember what my Dad taught me.

> "A raccoon has a ringed tail,
> a possum's tail is bare.
> A rabbit has no tail at all,
> just a little hunk of hair."

Chairman of the Board

In 1985, I was elected Chairman of the Board. I served as chairman through 1989. My number-one priority was to unload some of the "non-educational" situations that Dr. Beckes had gotten involved in. Dr. Beckes had a theory: that if someone needed a tax write-off and wanted to donate to Vincennes University—regardless of what it was—he took it. The worst example was several hundred acres of strip-mine waste. This was before the coal strip-mine companies had to leave their stripped ground in somewhat near the condition that they had started with. This donated ground we owned looked like a toxic nightmare.

The Cable Deal Finally Makes Money

We also owned a cambree-processing plant? What was it used for? That was my question. We also owned the Vincennes cable TV operation. This was not a gift. Dr. Beckes floated a million-dollar bond issue and had the Vincennes University employees wire the town. Vincennes sits in the middle of a triangle of Evansville, Terre Haute, and Bloomington. All three cities had a TV station, but the TV reception was iffy even with a roof-top antenna. To say our cable business was loosely run is an understatement. It was like Don's Guns. We didn't want to make any money: We just wanted to furnish a TV signal. The rates were way too low. The equipment was old. Very few houses bought a pay station, and there was no growth potential, seeing as how we had about 90-percent penetration.

I was a principal and on the board of American Cablevision in Indianapolis, so I had an idea of what it was worth. I suggested that we sell the cable operation. Despite some opposition, the board agreed. We hired a consultant from Denver who came up with nine interested parties. I told the board I thought we could get 10 million dollars. I really thought we could get 15 million dollars, and we ended up getting 19 million dollars. The board named our windfall The Endowment Fund, and the earnings went and are still going to scholarships, athletics, performing arts, etc.

Remember Who They Voted For

Governor O'Bannon was an admirer of Vincennes University. He was also a believer in community colleges. He proposed a community college plan that created a joint venture between Vincennes University and Ivy Tech. He appointed a committee to put together this partnership. I was appointed by O'Bannon to the committee. IU, from the Herman Wells days, has always been opposed to Indiana having a community college system. Herman Wells thought that the IU extensions filled that need.

While Governor O'Bannon was pushing for this community college concept, Myles Brand (from "I got rid of Bobby Knight" fame) openly opposed the concept. Brand even started pushing a remedial program at Indiana University. Here we have Indiana University, a research institution with world-famous schools of medicine, law, music, and business, and now he was going after students with 850–900 SAT scores who needed remedial help. These students would probably be thrown into large lecture classes taught by student assistants. Of course, accepting these students would give IU a larger head count, which meant more state dollars.

Now we have the governor promoting a program, with the president of a state-supported institution openly opposed to it. At one of our meetings, I pointed out that Steve Goldsmith had run and got quite a few votes from voters who wanted him to be our state chief executive officer and oversee our state's educational system. I pointed out that Frank O'Bannon had done the same thing and got more votes than Goldsmith to oversee our state's education system. But for the life of me, I couldn't remember Myles Brand getting even one vote to lead our whole state's higher-education policy.

The Bloomington newspaper printed my little analogy, and the next day, one of the IU trustees whom I knew, called and asked me to go to lunch with Brand. I did and found him to be more arrogant than I ever thought he was.

The Politics of Universities

After firing my favorite—Bobby Knight—Myles Brand

left IU for the NCAA. There was a strong push for Jim Morris to become President of IU. Jim Morris was an IU graduate and had been Chairman of the IU Board of Trustees. In my opinion, Jim would have made a great president. He would have made a great spokesman, and he had the capacity to raise lots of money for the university. And most of all, he's a Hoosier.

There was speculation that Jim (a former member of the Olympic Committee) helped Brand get the NCAA job. In any event, Jim Morris was not chosen to lead his alma mater. I heard a rumor that Steve Ferguson, a board member, was opposed to Morris because he had voted with Brand to fire Bobby Knight. Jim would have been a great president. We haven't had a president since John Ryan. John Ryan told me that when people asked him about Bobby Knight, he said, "When I go to bed at night, I can sleep. I don't worry about waking up the next morning and see on the TV that my university has been cheating on the NCAA rules."

With or without Myles Brand's opposition, we do have a community college system that is growing by leaps and bounds. Our current system provides college courses that are affordable and within commuting distance, regardless of where they live.

The marriage between Ivy Tech and Vincennes University just did not work for several reasons:

1. Vincennes University had made some early concessions, concerning what each institution would be responsible for, that were not helpful.

2. All of the classes would be held in Ivy Tech facilities.

3. Both Ivy Tech and Vincennes University wanted to pre-serve their independence as separate entities.

4. The head count became an issue in regards to who got credit for what.

5. Vincennes University had a tenured faculty.
   Ivy Tech did not.

6. Ivy Tech clearly had the muscle in the Legislature.

7. Stan Jones of the Higher Education Commission was afraid of the legislature if he didn't favor Ivy Tech.

8. Most of the members of the General Assembly worked for Ivy Tech.

Despite all the maneuvering by proponents of both institutions, things turned out for the best. Indiana now has a community college system that is working. Ivy Tech has a new innovative president, Tom Snyder, and it has record enrollments. Vincennes University has increased its enrollment, and has started several four-year baccalaureate programs in areas where there is a state-wide shortage, such as a four-year degree in nursing. Vincennes University, too, has a new, innovative president in Richard Helton. Both, I think, will work together in certain areas, and the state of Indiana now has affordable post-secondary education for all of its citizens.

We also still have Stan Jones running the Commission of Higher Education. He is a Democrat, who once served in the legislature, and ran unsuccessfully for Commissioner of Public Instruction. I understand he's still there because one of the Democrat members of his Board wants him to stay??? (Gosh, and I thought the Republicans won!)

A Good Place to Learn

Vincennes University will survive as it has done since 1801. It still has a niche. Its remedial programs are second to none. Every student is guaranteed individual attention by their instructors. Every member of the faculty, by contract, has to have office hours to meet with students who need help.

As a board member, and since then, I have suggested Vincennes University to literally hundreds of friends and acquaintances. I have seen young people with very-average or even low SAT scores go to Vincennes University, and after two years, go to a baccalaureate institution and excel there. The reason why they had an 800 SAT score was not because they were dumb or stupid: It was because they could not have cared less about school. They have been told they couldn't cut it. But they did cut it at Vincennes University. The light bulb came on.

Vincennes University also gets its share of excellent students with high SAT scores—some who just were not ready to go to an impersonal institution with thousands of freshman. Vincennes has graduates who have attended and did well at the best Ivy League schools. In the occupational areas for which Vincennes University is graduating students with associates degrees, people are getting high-paying jobs. There will always be a demand for institutions like Vincennes University.

Chapter 39
White River Park Commission

I was appointed to the White River Park Commission by Governor Bob Orr. I was on the commission when Evan Bayh was elected governor in 1989. Governor Bayh had appointed his young aides to have oversight on the various commissions. Bart Peterson, a nice young man, was the governor's representative for the White River Park Commission.

It was obvious that we were to have a new director. After all, new governor = new director. Young Mr. Peterson was informing us about how we were to advertise and interview for a new director. I said, "Look, Bart, tell us who the governor wants. I'm sure he has picked somebody, and we will elect him and save a whole lot of time and blood sugar for everyone."

Bart looked at me and said, "Mr. Early, I don't know how Republican governors do things, but my governor appoints good people on boards and commissions, and he trusts them to do their job. Whatever their decision is, he will accept that." I asked him whether he meant that the governor had no favorite for the job and that he would just accept anyone we chose. Bart said yes. I said, "Okay, I nominate Jack Crawford, a good Democrat who needs a job."

Jack Crawford, a really good attorney and a former prosecutor from Lake County, had been Evan's pick to head up the Hoosier Lottery. Jack had been accused of being too friendly with one of his female employees, and in addition to a whole lot of bad publicity, he had been fired as lottery director. When I nominated Jack (after all, he didn't have a job), Bart got a little nervous, whispered to the temporary director, who then called a "come back after lunch" recess. When we came back, we elected Evan's choice.

Appendix A

Potential Governors For 2012
Primary Elected Odds, Nevada Slim

Odds Potentials: Republican and One Democrat

5-1 **Republican Minority Leader Brian Bosma:**
Depends on the property tax issue. He has statewide
exposure and can raise money. Would have the
support of all "fundamentalist Christian" preachers,
and maybe even God.

5-1 **Marion County Prosecutor Carl Brizzi:** Can raise
money, but needs to work on statewide exposure.
Gets plenty of earned media in the important
Indianapolis TV market.

5-1 **Republican State Chairman Murray Clark:** Has
been the bridesmaid but never the bride. Has the
best rapport with the grass-roots organization, but
can they deliver? He can raise money. Does he want
it?

5-1 **Secretary of State Todd Rokita:** Sitting Secretary
of State. Probably can't depend on former IPL
directors for financial support but should have the
unqualified support of Bob Grand for raising money.
He will be working hard for the top spot and might
out-work all the others.

7-1 **Attorney General Steve Carter:** Hit a home run with his "Don't Call" list. Money might be the problem. Gets good P.R. from the media.

7-1 **State Senator Luke Kenley:** All depends on the property tax issue. If Joe Lunch Bucket likes it, he could be a contender. A Harvard graduate, he is smart.

8-1 **Congressman Steve Buyer:** A conservative who might want to jump from Congress to the governor's chair. Has name I.D. A Desert Storm veteran could probably raise the money.

8-1 **Senate President Pro Tem David Long:** Looks like a governor. Comes from a good money base (Fort Wayne) and has impressed the pros as an even-handed Pro-Tem. Like others from the Legislature, depends on the property tax issue.

8-1 **Super Bowl leader Mark Miles:** Was Dan Quayle's campaign manager when he ran for the senate. Runs with the Great-Big Dogs. Runs around with sophistisucks. Was MIA several years when he ran the World Tennis Association. Would be the darling of the establishment. Is really sharp and articulate. The Super Bowl hunt will give him lots of free media.

8-1 **Lt. Governor Becky Skillman:** High name I.D. Been a good spokesman for the Daniels team. Southern Indiana. Would run on Daniels' record.

10-1 **State Auditor Tim Berry:** A long-time state officeholder; great speaker; should have the unqualified support of Bob Grand for raising money. From Fort Wayne.

10-1 **State Treasurer Richard Murdoch:** State Treasurer from southern Indiana. Would appeal to the conservative Republicans. Should have the unqualified support of Bob Grand for raising the money.

10-1 **Congressman Mike Pence:** The darling of the conservatives. Has good name recognition in the Indianapolis media market. Never had to raise "big" money but could attract national money.

10-1 **State Senator Brent Steele:** Another conservative from southern Indiana. Would appeal to the Reagan-Independents and Democrats. If he could raise the money to be nominated, would run well in southern Indiana. As a legislator, has property tax as an issue.

15-1 **Mayor Greg Ballard:** Who knows? He might be the people's choice if he can solve the problems of Indianapolis. Should have the unqualified support of Bob Grand.

25-1 **Mayor Jim Brainard:** Carmel Mayor who could turn Indiana into one great roundabout. Should have the unqualified support of Bob Grand.

50-1 **Businessman Mickey Maurer:** A Democrat who now has been an advisor to both the Republican governor and Republican mayor. They might as well run him for governor. Would probably have the endorsement of the Indianapolis Business Journal and could self-finance his campaign. Did a great job as head of Economic Development for Gov. Mitch.

75-1 **The Field:** All the Republican legislators that are not mentioned.

7-5 **The odds that one of the big law firms will take credit for electing him or her:** Their backing might come late in the campaign.

Appendix B

My Top 10

George Jones
Tom T. Hall
Tony Stewart
General Chesty Puller, USMC
Bobby Knight
General George Patton
Ronald Reagan
Alex Clark
Henry D. Early
Bill Jenner

Hobbies

Bird and turkey hunting
Four-wheeling on my ATV
Shooting craps
NASCAR
Golf

My Favorite Place

The Hitching Post

Located in Jackson County on State Road 58, half-way between Kurtz and Heltonville. The food is great, especially their tenderloins. Every Friday night during the summer, there is a country music band that plays. On Saturday nights, they plan a game called Screw Your Neighbor. (Like French Lick, Screw Your Neighbor ain't what you might think. It's a pool game.)

The End

I could tell some other stories, but the Statute of Limitations
might not have expired.
And besides that, I am saving them for my next book.
Now I've got to get back to my rat killing.

Index

F

Fagg, Robert 2, **153**
Ford, Gerald 65
Fox News Channel 169
Freeland, Dick 168, 171
French, Darrell 171, 280
French, Ed 115
Frenzel III, Otto 254
Frick, Dave 105

G

Galloway, Jim 2
Garrison, Greg 196
Garton, Bob 146, 199, 201, 289
Gates, Bob 73
Geist, Ray 191
George 56
Gifford, Pat 116
Gingrich, Newt **161**, 180
Giuliani, Rudy 165
Gohmann, Bud 82, 91-97, 132, 176, 187, 214, 243, 259
Goldsmith, Steve 106, 114, 134-135, 145-148, 165-167, 170-173, 295
Grand, Bob 301, 303
Grandstiff, Jean 169
Gregg, John 259, 290
Grills, Nelson 197
Guthrie, Dick 40

H

Haldeman, Bob 54
Hamilton, David 180, 183
Hamilton, Lee 197
Handley, Harold 69, 202
Hanna, Larry 99, 102
Harbaugh, Jim 167-168
Harcourt, Jean Ann 120, 129, 168
Harden, Cecil 235
Harrison, William Henry 287-289
Hartke, Vance 54, 85
Hasbrook, Tom 254
Helmke, Paul 136

H

Hemphill, Doc 73-74
Hesseldenz, Jack 75, 82, **162**, 225, 242, 273
Hibbes, Gene 255
Hibner, Janet 180
Hiler, Bob 120, 129
Hiler, Jack 180
Hill, Dub 52
Hill, Margie 120
Hodawald, John 106
Holder, Cale 30, 67-69, 71, 233
Holland, Gladys 107
Hubbard, Al 122, 133-136, 146
Hudnut, Bill 44, 56, 99-106, 114, **153**, 187
hully-gully(s) ix, 45, 88, 104, 135, 257-259, 261, 271
Huse, Judge Frank 94

I

Indiana Society 279-282
Indiana University 22
Indiana Week in Review 141-145
Indianapolis Cablevision 254-255
The Indianapolis Foundation 106, 283-286
The Indianapolis Star 30, 40, 56, 61-62, 68, 92, 96, 102, 104-105, 134, 165-166, 188, 201, 211-214, 222, 225
Indianapolis Water Company 48, 221
Irsay, Nancy (Bob) 171

J

Jacobs, Andy 197
Jenner, Bill 3, 30, 65-70, 148, 202, 235, 305
Jennings, Jonathon 288
Jimison, Z. Mae 147
Johnson, Kathleen 165, 212
Jontz, Jim 128
Julian Center iii, 144

K

Kaufman, Ron 192
Keating, Tom 188
Kenley, Luke 302
Kersey, Sharyn 127, 169
Kissinger, Henry **162**
Kittle, James **163**
Knall, Dave 255
Knight, Bobby 147, 295-296, 305
Kuntz, Tom 225
Kuykendall, Rufus 48

L

Lamkin, Martha 78
law firms 68, 86, 199, 204-212,
  216, 304
Lewis, Ed iii, 59, 85-86, 130, 213-219
Lieberman, Senator Joe 131
Lightle, Susie 127, 169
Lilly, Eli 283
Little Sisters of the Poor 94-95, 201,
  207, 285
Lloyd, Dr. Frank 53, 255
Long, David 302
Longworth, Nick 187
Lugar, Bertha 45
Lugar, Richard 5, 43-52, 55, 87-89,
  153, 191, 201
Luse, Keith 113, 116-117

M

Magnason, Claude 280
Maio, Mike 57, 57-58, 231-234
Mann, Jerry and Edna 192
Mannweiller, Paul 114
Marco Island 97, 113, **161**, 236
Marion County 24, 29-31, 33-38,
  40-41, 44, 49, 53-54, 56, 61-63, 71,
  73, 91, 94-95, 117, 137, 147, 186,
  196-197, 200, 202-203, 205, 207,
  213-215, 223, 235-236, 243, 255,
  261, 269, 280, 283-284, 301

Marshall, Ruth 24, 34
Mars Hill 45
Martin, Wendell 41
Matalin, Mary 121
Maurer, Mickey 303
Mawrey, Sheila 133
Maxum, Bill 235
Maxwell, Elsworth 25-26
McAllister, P.E. 254
McCarthy, Joe 3, 67, 70
McCarthy, Shawn 169
McCloskey, Frank 80, 179
McDaniel, Mike 103, 137, **160**
  163, 215, 258-259
McGovern, George **159**
McIntosh, David 122, 138, 168
McIntyre, Rick 80, 179
McKinney Jr., Frank 47, 105,
  124, 222, 254, 281
McKinney Sr., Frank 45, 124
McNutt, Paul 283
Meese, Ed 110
Miles, Mark 302
Miller, Eric 148
Miller, Glenn 267
Miller, Pat 119
Miller, Sol 27
Miller, Tom 106
Moran, Sarah 1
Morris, Jim 47, 51, 296
Morris, Marty 5, 88
Moses, Tom 221
mummy-dummy(s) 185, 187,
  261-262
Murdoch, Richard 303
Mussolini, Benito 45
Mutz, John 58, 103, 130, 144,
  213, 215-216
Myer, Runt 12
myrmidon 166, 261-262